How To Use a
Research Library

How To Use a Research Library

David Beasley

New York   Oxford
OXFORD UNIVERSITY PRESS
1988

Oxford University Press

Oxford   New York   Toronto
Delhi   Bombay   Calcutta   Madras   Karachi
Petaling Jaya   Singapore   Hong Kong   Tokyo
Nairobi   Dar es Salaam   Cape Town
Melbourne   Auckland

and associated companies in
Berlin   Ibadan

Published by Oxford University Press, Inc.
200 Madison Avenue, New York, New York 10016

Oxford is a registered trademark of Oxford University Press

Library of Congress Cataloging-in-Publication Data

Beasley, David R., 1931–
   How to use a research library.

Includes index.
   1. Research libraries—Handbooks, manuals, etc.
2. Library orientation—Handbooks, manuals, etc.
3. Bibliography—Methodology—Handbooks, manuals, etc.
4. Research—Methodology—Handbooks, manuals, etc.
Z675.R45B42   1988   025.5′677   87-14024
ISBN 0-19-504245-X
ISBN 0-19-504246-9 (pbk.)

9 8 7 6 5 4 3 2 1

Printed in the United States of America
on acid-free paper

Acknowledgments

My heartfelt thanks to William Coakley for valuable editorial advice.

Material from the following figures in this book were made possible by the kind permission of their respective publishers and representatives:

Fig. 7a—From page 1920 of *Cumulative Book Index* 1977, January–December 1977. Copyright © 1977, 1978 by The H. W. Wilson Company. Material reproduced by permission of the publisher.

Fig. 7d—From page 299, 1979 edition of the *PAIS Bulletin.* Reprinted by permission of the publisher.

Fig. 7e—From page 1037 of *Cumulative Book Index* 1983, January–December 1983. Copyright © 1983, 1984 by The H. W. Wilson Company. Material reproduced by permission of the publisher.

Figs. 3.4 and 3.5—Reproduced from Henry, Leigh, Tedd and Williams, *Online Searching An Introduction* 1980, pp. 20 and 91 by permission of the publishers, Butterworths and Co. Publishers Ltd.

Fig. 4.1—Entry from The New York Times Index (Quinn–1960). Copyright © 1960 by The New York Times Company. Reprinted by permission.

All figures containing material from the New York Public Library are reprinted by permission of the Library.

**For Marie Nicholas
and in fond memory of
Aloysius Nicholas**

Preface

This short book is for the college student, the casual researcher, and the professional researcher and writer. Those unfamiliar with libraries should read from page one; those more experienced can go directly to particular sections outlined in the Contents.

The examples I have chosen to clarify research procedures in libraries are taken largely from The Research Libraries of The New York Public Library. Procedures are basically the same for all research libraries; they differ in minor ways, such as in the form of request slip or kind of catalog. At the end of the book I note some of the differences I have encountered in other major research libraries.

There are many levels of research and many different kinds of facts you will need to know. This work will have served its purpose admirably if it helps you apply the most efficient methods of library research to find the bibliographical tools most useful to your own particular needs.

New York City   D.R.B.
May 1987

Contents

How To Use a
Research Library

Quick Reference Guide

HOW TO OBTAIN A BOOK OR PERIODICAL

This section is a brief overview for those of you who want to locate a publication in the library right away or need a quick review of the essentials. Chapter 1 begins a detailed initiation into the use of research libraries. Specific examples and references throughout this book are to The Research Libraries of The New York Public Library (NYPL), but the general procedures are similar in all research libraries.

Following are some points to keep in mind about using a reference section:

1. Books and periodicals are to be consulted in the Research Libraries only. You cannot borrow them.
2. There are several catalogs and many ways of finding publications; some you can find only by asking the librarian (for further details, see p. 22).
3. To make a photocopy from a publication, you must obtain a pass from the librarian to take it from the reading room to the photoservice section.
4. Do not despair of finding the publication you want. If the library does not have it available through the catalogs or in deferred status or microform, the librarian can obtain it for you from another library, or give you a METRO pass to see it in a library within the metropolitan area (see p. 89).
5. When you have located the publication in a library card, do not forget to write down the call number on the request slip.
6. To use the Special Collections for rare or manuscript materials (e.g., Print Collection, Rare Book Room, Manuscripts and Archives, Berg

Collection), you must obtain a pass from the Office of Special Collections.

Requesting a Publication

When you enter the NYPL Central Research Library, ask the librarian at the Information Desk to the left of the main entrance on Fifth Avenue to guide you to the division where the publications you want are located. If you want a reference work, such as an almanac, directory, or encyclopedia, the librarians at the reference desks can tell you where you can take it off the open shelves in the reading rooms. This saves you from using the library catalogs.

Any issue of a periodical that appeared within the year is on the current periodical shelves, where you can request it without a call number. But books and issues of periodicals no longer current are in bound form in the stacks or on microform in the microform reading areas. To request these you must find their call numbers in the library's catalogs or in special bibliographies and indices that act as catalogs (see p. 32). You find books on your subject by looking in the catalogs under the correct subject heading. Ask a librarian if you have any trouble locating an appropriate heading.

The call number or classmark identifies the location of the publication in the library. (It is listed at the top righthand corner of a catalog card entry or in boldface on the bottom line of a recent book or computer entry.) Write down the author and title on a request slip with the call number for a book or microform, (Fig. 1). For a serial (e.g., a periodical or an annual report), include only the periodical's title and the date of the issue with the call number (Fig. 2). For an annual report or similar serial, write down the corporate author and title (see p. 36) (Fig. 3).

Different catalogs span different years. If the book you are looking for was published prior to 1970, you can probably find it listed in the NYPL *Dictionary Catalog of The Research Libraries, 1911–1971* (black volumes; referred to hereafter as NYPL *Dictionary Catalog, 1911–1971*). If it was published between 1970 and 1980 you can probably find it in the NYPL Research Libraries' *Dictionary Catalog* [1972–80] (blue volumes) or its *Supplement* [1972–80] (red volumes). Books published later you can find in the NYPL Research Libraries' *Interim List: Index* or through the online computer terminal, CATNYP, which

The New York
Public Library   Call number: $S\ H\ H$
ASTOR, LENOX AND TILDEN FOUNDATIONS

Author or
Periodical: *Ford Foundation*

Book Title: *Annual Report*

Date/Vol. No.: *1980*

Correct and Legible Name and Address Required

Name *Mary Jackson*   Seat number:

Address *31 Main St.*   *72*

City *NY NY*   Zip

School or Business *Allardyce Inc*

form 28s

Fig. 3

cites publications cataloged in recent years (see p. 43 for a description of how to use it). Some works are listed only in special division or format catalogs (see p. 53); ask a librarian for help if you do not find a work listed in the main catalogs.

Requesting a Book:

1. It is always easier to locate a book in most catalogs if you know the author's name. When you know only the title or subject, use a general bibliography like *Cumulative Book Index* or *Books in Print* (see p. 48) to find the author. The NYPL *Dictionary Catalog, 1911–1971* also lists works under subject headings, and sometimes under title.

2. If you find a book in the NYPL *Dictionary Catalog, 1911–1971* by subject heading or added entry, such as a joint author, write down only the main entry where the request slip requires the author and the title or a condensed version, using the first few words (see Figs. 4a and b, 5a and b). Books are located by their main entries within the call numbers (see p. 60).

   If you request books from the NYPL Research Libraries' *Dictionary Catalog* [1972–80], its *Supplement*, or the *Interim List*, and the entry confuses you, you do not need to use the main entry on

Title

Main entry

Subject entry

**CHURCHILL, SIR WINSTON LEONARD
SPENCER, 1874–**

*C–4 pv.773

Canadian club of Toronto.
Canada's tribute to Sir Winston Churchill on the eve of his
eightieth birthday; the Canadian club of Toronto dinner meeting,
Royal York hotel, November 29th, 1954. [Toronto, 1954] 22 p.
illus., ports.   25cm.

1. Churchill, Sir Winston Leonard Spencer, 1874–
NN**RX 2.58   OS PC, 1 SL E1 (LC1, X1)

Fig. 4a

Title
Main entry
Subject heading

GREAT BRITAIN–POLITICS, 1945–

CM

CHURCHILL, Sir WINSTON LEONARD SPENCER, 1874–
In the balance; speeches 1949 and 1950...ed. by Randolph S.
Churchill. Boston, Houghton Mifflin co., 1952. x, 456 p. 22cm.

1. Great Britain–Politics, 1945–   . 2. Great Britain–For. rel.,
1945–   .3. European federation, 1939–   . 4. World politics,
1945–   . I. Churchill, Randolph Spencer, 1911–   , ed.
II. Title.
NN*R X 12.54 g/x OCs, IS PCs, 1s, 2, 3s, 4s, Is, IIs SLs
Es, 1s, 2, 3s 4s, Is, IIs (LC1s, X1s)

Fig. 5a

The New York Public Library
ASTOR, LENOX AND TILDEN FOUNDATIONS

Call number: C M

Author or Periodical: *Churchill, Winston*

Book Title: *In the balance*

Date/Vol. No.:

Correct and Legible Name and Address Required

Name *John Smith*

Address *19 Rivermore Rd.*

City *Bronx, N.Y.* Zip _____

School or Business *Fordham University*

Seat number:

35

form 28s

the request slip; simply write the call number, which represents a fixed location. If you are ordering a particular volume, do not forget to include the volume number (Fig. 6).

If you are looking for a very recently published book, go directly to the library's computer catalog (CATNYP). It includes all the entries (books, pamphlets, periodicals) in the book catalogs covering 1972 to date, plus cataloged items acquired too recently to be in these catalogs. Just type f/a (for "find author"), f/t (for "find

La chute d'Icare. ◄─────────────────────────── Title added entry
• Menant, Sylvain. ◄──────────────────────── Main entry
   La chute d'Icare : la crise de la poesie
francaise 1700−1750 / Sylvain Menant. −Geneve ──── Title
: Droz, 1981.
   395 p. ; 23 cm. − (Histoire des idees et
critique litteraire ; no 193) ◄──────────────── Monograph series
■■JFE 81−2372. ◄────────────────────────── and number
                                          ────────── Call number

The New York Public Library Call number: JFE 81−2372

Author or Periodical:

Book Title:

Date/Vol. No.:

Correct and Legible Name and Address Required

Name _Mary Jackson_   Seat number:
Address _31 Main_
City _NYC_   Zip _10007_   _72_
School or Business _Allardyce Inc._   form: 30a

Fig. 6 Analyzed series title. The dot before the main entry indicates that the book is not cataloged by series. The call number alone will get you the book.

title''), f/a and f/t, or f/s (for ''find subject''), then the author, title, or subject, and press the return key to bring the cataloged information to the monitor screen. The computer guides you (see p. 44).

3. If the book is a volume in a numbered monograph series and it has not been analyzed in the catalogs (i.e., you cannot find it by author or monograph title), you may find the title of the series in the catalogs. Request the series and the number of the volume you wish to see. You can obtain the number by looking up the author, subject, or title in the *Cumulative Book Index* (Fig. 7a through f) (see pp. 10–12).

Requesting a periodical article:

1. To find the title and date of the periodical in which an article appears, you look in the periodical indexes that cover the subject of the article. If you know the magazine in which the article appeared,

Fig. 7a The CBI (Cumulative Book Index) gives you the number of the monographic series by author and title of the pamphlet or book you want to find in the library catalog. In this case, under author, Price, David Lynn, you find the series "Washington papers. v 4, no41."

```
Price. Cecil John Layton
   Gwyn Jones (pub for) the Welsh Arts Council.
     (Writers of Wales) limited ed Q 72p £10 '76
     University of Wales Press
     LC 76-375928
   (ed) See Sheridan, R. B. B. Plays
Price. Christine. 1928-
   Arts of clay. 64p il lib bdg $6.95 '77 Scribner
     ISBN 0-684-15120-0    LC 77-23103
   Arts of wood. 64p il maps lib bdg $6.95 '76 Scrib-
     ner
     ISBN 0-684-14665-7    LC 76-13886
Price. David Lynn
   Oil and Middle East security. (Georgetown Univ.
     Center for Strategic and Int. Studies. Wash-
     ington papers. v4 no41) 84p pa $3 '76 Sage
     Publications
     ISBN 0-8038-0791-5    LC 76-54450
```

Fig. 7b You find the series in the library catalog from number one followed by a dash ("1–   ").

Main
entry

The Washington papers. 1- Beverly Hills [etc.]
Sage Publications [etc.] 1977- 22 cm. CURRENT
ISSUES AVAILABLE IN ECONOMICS AND PUBLIC
AFFAIRS DIVISION. FULL RECORD OF
HOLDINGS IN CENTRAL SERIAL RECORD.
Irregular, 1977-79; 8 no. a year, 1980- "Published for the
Center for Strategic and International Studies,
Georgetown University."   NN 80-4857398
                                          [JLK 80-156]   Call
                                                                  number

Fig. 7d Sometimes the CBI does not pick up a publication when it should.
You cannot find a publication on SALT and security by David Yost in CBI,
so you turn to the PAIS *Bulletin* (which covers political subjects) and look it
up under the subject heading in the volume covering the year of its
publication, 1981. You find that it is in the series "Washington papers, no.
85" and request it accordingly.

STRATEGIC AIR COMMAND. See United States - Air
force - Strategic air command.

STRATEGIC ARMS LIMITATION TALKS

Cutler, Lloyd N. and Roger C. Molander. Is there life
after death for SALT? *Internat Security 6:3-20 Fall '81*

† Gray, Colin S. and Keith B. Payne. SALT: deep force
level reductions; final report. Mr '81 v.p. (HI-3195-RR)
pa Nonprofit agencies $20; others, price on request
—*Hudson inst*
   Prepared for the SALT/Arms Control Support
Group, U.S. Office of the Assistant to the Secretary of
Defense (Atomic Energy).
   Feasibility of reductions of strategic force in SALT
III.

† Lehman, John F. and Seymour Weiss. Beyond the Salt II
failure; foreword by Richard Perle. '81 xxi+195p tables
index (Praeger Special Studies/Praeger Sci.) (LC
81-2874) (ISBN 0-03-059448-0) $23.95—*Praeger pub*

Sharp, Jane M. O. Restructuring the SALT dialogue.
Internat Security 6:144-76 Winter '81/'82

Yost, David S. European security and the SALT process;
foreword by Uwe Nerlich. '81 96p bibl (Washington ◄——— series
Pa. 85) (Sage Policy Pa.) (LC 81-52788) (ISBN
0-8039-1739-2) pa $4—*Sage pubns*
   Published for the Center for Strategic and
International Studies, Georgetown University.

11

Fig. 7e You may look in CBI under author or title and find the series that includes the publication, but you cannot find the series in the library catalog. This is because the library you happen to be using decided to keep this series as an SID (Subject for Individual Decision). SID means that the library collects only selected monographs from that series. These monographs may be found in the library catalog usually by author or title, not by series. Here are two examples of monographic series kept as SIDs.

> **Heat transfer in nuclear reactor safety**; edited by S. George
> Bankoff and N.H. Afgan. (Proceedings of the Inter-
> national Centre for Heat and Mass Transfer. 13) 964p ◄──
> il 1982 Hemisphere
> ISBN 0-89116-223-2   LC 81-13333
>   Papers delivered at the Int. Centre for Heat and
> Mass Transfer Seminar on Nuclear Reactor Safety Heat
> Transfer in Dubrovnik. Yugoslavia. Sept. 1-5, 1980
> **Heat-transfer media**
>   *See also*
>   Heat pipes
> **Heat treater's guide**: standard practices and procedures for
> steel: edited by Paul M. Unterweiser. Howard E. Boyer.
> James J. Kubbs. Q 493p il 1982 American Soc. for
> Metals
> ISBN 0-87170-141-3   LC 82-8680
> **Heat treatment of steel** *See* Steel—Heat treatment
> **Heat treatment, structure, and properties of nonferrous alloys.**
> Brooks. C. R. 1982 American Soc. for Metals
> **Heater, Homer**
> A Septuagint translation technique in the Book of Job:
> by Homer Heater. Jr. (Catholic Biblical quarterly.
> Monograph series. 11) 152p pa 1982 Catholic Biblical ◄──
> Assn. of Am.
> ISBN 0-915170-10-8   LC 81-10085

Fig. 7f No. 13 of the Proceedings on the International Centre for Heat and Mass Transfer is found only under the title entry in the library catalog.

> *Heat transfer in nuclear reactor safety / —
> Hemisphere Pub. Corp., c1982. xii, 964 p. : ill.
> Reg. no.: 0174802
> **Call no.: JSE 83-225**

look in *Ulrich's International Periodicals Directory* to see if the magazine is indexed and by which periodical service.

2. Most periodical indexes list by subject. Some, such as the *Readers' Guide to Periodical Literature,* index by author as well. Note for yourself the page numbers of the article within the volume (and the author and title of the article, if you will not remember it). Enter on the request slip *only* the title of the periodical and the date of the article (Fig. 8a on p. 13 and 8b on p. 14).

3. To find the call number for a periodical, first check whether a handy

reference file to periodicals exists from which you can get the call numbers. If you do not find it in the handy file, look in the library catalogs. You should know that libraries catalog only the first number of a series; they leave an open entry (e.g., v. 1–■), indicating successive volumes added to the first when they are received. Therefore, if you want a 1980 volume of a periodical that began publication in 1920, you would find its call number in the NYPL *Dictionary Catalog, 1911–71*. If the periodical began in 1974 it

ECONOMIC ASSISTANCE
  See also
  Arab states - Economic assistance program
  Belgium - Economic assistance program.
  Canada - Economic assistance program.
  China (People's Republic) - Economic assistance program.
  Europe, Western - Economic assistance program.
  European economic community - Economic assistance
    program.
  Finland - Economic assistance program.
  Germany, West - Economic assistance program
  International bank for reconstruction and development.
  International development association.
  Israel - Economic assistance program.
  Netherlands - Economic assistance program.
  Organization of petroleum exporting countries -
    Economic assistance program.
  Technical assistance.
  United Nations - Development program
  United States - Economic assistance program.

  Baqai, Moinuddin. A new framework for international
    financial co-operation for development. *Trade and
    Development* p 39-51 Spring '79 this issue $8

  Betts, T. F. Development aid from voluntary agencies to
    the least developed countries. *Africa Today* 25:49-68
    O/D '78
      Adapted and updated from a document prepared
    under commission from the United Nations conference
    for trade and development, 1977.

  † Bijli, Shah M. Development aid. '79 xii + 103p bibl tables   ◀━━━
    index Rs 38—*Shree publishing house, 4056, Ajmeri
    Gate, Delhi-110006, India*
      Overall picture of the concept of aid and the various
    forms assistance has taken.

  Bird, Graham. An integrated programme for finance and
    aid: shortcomings in the existing arrangements for
    providing the developing countries with finance and aid
    could be met by establishing a new international
    development organisation funded through the creation
    of SDRs [special drawing rights], thus introducing a
    link between the creation of international liquidity and
    the provision of aid. *Banker (London) 129:87+ S '79*   ◀━━━

Fig. 8a   Note that the "Bijli, Shah M." entry is a book. You can tell by form of pagination, that is, "103p." Look it up in the catalog by author. In the entry for "Bird, Graham," you can tell it is a periodical article because the last line indicates: *Banker* Sept. 1979 (v.129, p.87).

will be listed in the blue NYPL Research Libraries' *Dictionary Catalog* [1972–80]. If it began publication in the past year or two, it may not yet be entered in the catalogs, but you may find it in the current periodical section.

Filing Request Slips

In the General Research Division (Room 315)
After you have filled out the request slip with call number, author, title (and date or volume number if necessary), and your name and address, take it to the file clerk at the reference desk. The clerk will give you a card with a number on it and directions to proceed to the light indicators either in the North or the South Reading Hall. When your number lights up on the indicator board, present your card to the clerk behind the counter and you will receive the material you requested, or your slip will be returned with directions explaining why you did not receive the material (see p. 50).

In the Subject Divisions or Special Collections
Before you hand your request slip to a librarian, you must select a seat number from a table in the reading rooms and write this number in

the lower righthand corner of the request slip. A library page will bring the material to you at your seat. (This is the procedure followed in the main reading rooms of the British Library and the Bibliothèque Nationale.)

PUBLICATIONS IN MICROFORM

If the material you want has a call number starting with *Z − , it is on microfilm. If the call number begins with *X-, it is on microfiche. If the call number does not indicate it is held by a subject division, you request this material in the microform reading area in the North Reading Hall, Room 315M. There is also a microform reading room at the back of the Economic and Public Affairs Division (Room 229M) and microform readers in other subject divisions, such as the Jewish Division, the Slavonic Division, the Schomburg Center, and divisions of the Performing Arts Research Center (see pp. 126–129), for reading microform materials kept in those divisions.

Much of the material on microform is not cataloged. You must use special bibliographic tools to obtain them. Ask a librarian for guidance (see p. 58).

INTERLIBRARY LOAN

The Cooperative Services section in Room 315 can obtain a book from another library for you if NYPL does not have it. (For sources to check, see p. 86.) You can also arrange here for articles from periodicals not in the library to be reproduced in other libraries and forwarded to you at NYPL. (Up to 50 pages are done free of charge.)

ONLINE SEARCHING

The information you need is sometimes best found in a computer data base, rather than a book or periodical. The librarian interviews you to determine whether online searching should be used, which data base should be contacted, and how much money you wish to spend in the search.

In the United States there are three major network lines: Telenet, Tymnet, and Uninet. Their host services, such as Dialog, and the data banks these services provide in North America and abroad (through Euronet) are multifarious and complicated (see p. 93 for details).

LIBRARIANS AND HOW TO DEAL WITH THEM

"When I go into a bank, I get rattled," a Stephen Leacock story begins. "The clerks rattle me. . . ." The same could often be said about research libraries and librarians.

So the first thing you must learn is to overcome any hesitancy in approaching librarians; they are subject specialists trained to direct you to the correct sources for using the collections. Research librarians not only hold advanced degrees in library science, but often advanced degrees in another field, making them subject specialists in that field as well. As you become familiar with the library and its staff, you will get to know which librarians have the special skills you need to help you in your particular areas of interest. Be explicit in describing your information needs to the librarians. Because librarians are often hard-pressed for time, you should formulate your questions carefully before you ask them. Your ability to describe your research needs clearly enables librarians to give you the full benefit of their knowledge and training. Actually, if you follow the advice of this book, your greater library knowledge will increase the librarians' cooperation and respect for you as a serious researcher.

The procedures for finding materials in large research libraries are more involved than those for smaller libraries. But the first thing to remember is that the research is *your* responsibility. Research librarians are not there to do your work for you, but to direct you to the reference sources where you will find the facts required for your specific subject areas of research. This should not prevent you from asking questions in pursuit of your research, however, for most of what you need can be found in any modern research library.

RULES AND HOW TO DEAL WITH THEM

For the most part, researchers do not know the rules of library procedure until they break one. The rules exist for the practical purpose of protecting the collection as well as controlling the location and retrieval of the books, periodicals, manuscripts, and other works in the extensive stack areas and reading rooms of a large reference library. At most research libraries you cannot carry books from one division to another, or from outside the library into the main reading room, without a special pass. At some libraries, readers need passes to enter special divisions or to use pens, typewriters, and recording equipment.

Some rules can be bent. If you find your ability to pursue your research is obstructed by a particular library rule, explain your needs to the librarian and ask if an exception can be made in your case. The librarian will try to accommodate you if at all possible. One rule, however, remains steadfast—the prohibition against borrowing or removing books from most research libraries. But you can usually photocopy materials essential to your work.

1

General Approach to the Research Library

Elementary, my dear Watson

WHAT A RESEARCH LIBRARY OFFERS

A research library is an extensive storehouse of information classified for quick retrieval. Several large research libraries have holdings covering all subjects—the New York Public Library, the Library of Congress, the British Library, and the Bibliothèque Nationale, for example. It is these libraries that concern us in this book. Hundreds of smaller research libraries collect only in certain subject or language areas. These have to be used almost exclusively when research is done on specific subjects, such as theology, medicine, and law. Other important research libraries are university libraries, which shape their collections to the needs of their students and faculty.

What does a research library do for you that a branch library cannot do?

A research library does three things: (1) it provides depth of information; it keeps many books on a subject, including all scholarly works, whereas most branch libraries have room for only a few select books that are popular; (2) it provides an historical view: a research library keeps one copy of most works as a permanent record, so that you can find almost everything published on a given subject, whereas a branch library discards older books to make room for the latest books on a subject; and finally (3) it aims at comprehensiveness: a research library collects widely all forms of publications, whereas the branch library is restricted to collecting materials that can circulate and selecting only a small reference and periodical section to meet the needs of the local community it serves.

WHERE TO BEGIN

Can you get information from a research library without visiting the library?
Most research libraries provide a telephone information service that answers those questions a librarian can research within minutes.

Moreover, the use of information-retrieval systems in the home or office, although expensive, is becoming widespread. Your telephone or television set can be hooked up to several data bases, which can type out brief, factual replies to your questions. For research demanding more than simple facts, however, you must visit the library.

What do you do first when you enter a research library?
Most research libraries require a reader's pass, which you can acquire (sometimes for a fee) at the Administrative Office; in the Bibliothèque Nationale of Paris, for example, you must provide a passport-size photograph of yourself. At The New York Public Library (except for Special Collections) and the Library of Congress in Washington, D.C., however, readers' passes are not required.

Some research libraries, such as NYPL, have separate subject or form departments: art, economics, genealogy, microforms, science, and others. You go to the Central Information Desk to get directions to the department that covers your subject. Other libraries—the British Library in London, for example—have one main reading room with separate departments only for keeping materials such as government publications, manuscripts, and rare books.

On entering the reading rooms what sort of responses to your questions can you expect from the reference librarian?
The librarian may have to ask you for more details, or may rephrase your question to get a better understanding of what you are seeking. Then you can be directed to a specific section in a specific area, as follows:

Reference Shelf Area. (1) To find a list of books on a particular subject, a bibliography is recommended. (2) For a biographic sketch, appropriate biographical dictionaries or the *Biography Index* are suggested. (3) For the address of a company, a directory of corporations is useful. (4) The U.S. population census for 1980 can be found on the open shelves. (5) To find out how much water flows over Niagara Falls, a ready-reference almanac can be used. (6) And to find a periodical article on a certain subject, the correct periodical indices are the source.

Catalog Area. (1) To find a book by a certain author, you can use the library catalogs (see the Quick Reference Guide for a quick summary of procedures for finding classmarks or call numbers and filling out request slips). (2) For more biographical information about a person than is provided by the biographical directories on the reference-room shelves, the librarian may suggest checking the library catalogs under the person's name as subject. (3) If you cannot find books in the catalogs under a certain subject, perhaps the catalogers used a different subject heading, in which case the librarian can suggest other headings from the subject heading guide. (4) Finally, if you want back issues of a periodical or an annual corporation manual, the librarian can help you find the classmark by directing you to the catalogs that list the series.

Data-bank Area. (1) For complete bibliographic information on a specific subject quickly, the librarian can hook into the appropriate computer data bank and obtain the bibliographic printout for a fee (some of the library's own computer records may be available free). (2) To obtain facts on a news event within the past 10 years immediately, the librarian can contact a newspaper's data banks in storage-retrieval for a fee.

Special Collections Area. To find a rare book, an author's manuscript, the correspondence of a politician, or an Audubon print, the librarian directs you to the Special Collections Office for a pass to visit the particular Special Collection you need.

What are the reference works and how do you find them?
Reference works are dictionaries, directories, encyclopedias, almanacs, biographical works, standard editions, bibliographies, periodical indices, and other aids for finding information in the collection. They are self-contained—they have their own indices and give basic information without requiring you to seek further. These books are usually cataloged with the call number prefix ''R − .''

Reference works are available for use on the open shelves of the reading rooms, whereas the bulk of the research collection is on closed shelves, from which (in most research libraries) the books can be retrieved only by library personnel.

2
Catalogs and How To Use Them

What is a catalog?
A catalog is a record of the publications the library holds in its collection. It guides you to the specific publication you are looking for.

How many forms of catalogs are there?
Catalogs come in four forms. (1) card catalogs, in which each card represents a separate publication; (2) book catalogs, in which sometimes the entries are printed and other times the cards from the card catalog are photocopied; (3) microfilm catalogs, which can be used with a microform viewer; and (4) online catalogs, which are seen on a computer terminal screen and operated by a keyboard.

What is your object in consulting the catalogs?
First, you want to see if the library has the particular book you are looking for as well as any other books on the subject you are researching.

Second, to retrieve the book or books from the library stacks, you must make out a request slip provided by the library by printing the name of the author, title, and classmark given in the catalog.

The following sections describe how to use the card catalog, dictionary catalog, microform catalog, and online catalog.

CARD CATALOGS

Card catalogs are arranged or filed alphabetically by author, subject, and title. For example, for an author named James Finance, all the books by him would be entered in the card catalog on cards each containing his name and then the title of one of his books, thus:

Finance, James, 1921–1970.
  Country talk . . .

Behind the books written by James Finance are books he has compiled, edited, or coauthored, for example:

Finance, James, 1921–1970, ed.
  Diamond, Alex, 1912–1960.
    The Jubilee years . . .

Next come cards for books about James Finance, that is, biographies, reminiscences, and critical works:

Finance, James, 1921–1970.
  Jackson, Abel, 1930–
    Jimmie Finance, my old pal . . .

or

Finance, James, 1921–1970.
  Addison, Joseph, 1926–
    The Narrative style of James Finance . . .

Following these are cards for books by other authors named Finance such as "Finance, Zeke," and then cards with the subject heading FINANCE, followed by cards on which the subject heading is regionalized, that is, FINANCE—FRANCE. Finally, come publications with the title Finance, such as the periodical *Finance* (London) v.1 no.1– May 1950–

Filing Quirks

Remember that titles are filed after subject headings; otherwise, you may become lost in the thousands of subject-heading cards and think the library does not have the periodical you want. By remembering this arrangement—that is, *author, subject, title*—you can find your way through the catalog with ease.

Three simple filing rules will help you locate books in the catalog:

1. Cards are filed word by word not letter by letter: "New York," for example follows "New Haven" and precedes "New Zealand," but all three precede "Newport" and "Newspaper."
2. Cards with abbreviated capital letters standing for companies or institutions, such as IBM, are found at the beginning of the file for

each letter, that is, IBM comes at the beginning of the "I's," preceding "Iago," for example.
3. In some catalogs "Mc" (as in "McNabb") is filed as if it were "Mac" (as in "MacNabb").

Locating Series Volumes or Other Parts of Works

Analyzed Monograph Series

It is important to know how to find a monograph published in a series because you encounter these series often in the most elementary research, and library catalogs index them in different ways.

First, the American Library Association defines a series as "A number of separate works, usually related to one another in subject or otherwise, issued in succession, normally by the same publishers and in uniform style, with a collective title which generally appears at the head of the title page, on the half-title, or on the cover."

Unnumbered volumes in a monograph series are cataloged as though they are published individually. Numbered volumes in a monograph series issued by a corporate body or institution, however, are given separate catalog entries yet kept as part of the series. The cataloger provides a separate card under the author for a particular monograph in a series. For example, we find under Sir Winston Churchill a monograph he coauthored with Franklin Roosevelt and Mordecai Ezekiel (Fig. 2.1). (Cards for this monograph are also filed under Roosevelt and Ezekiel.)

To request this monograph, you would follow the instructions in the top righthand corner of the card: "Write on slip words underlined and classmark" *only*. Thus, you would write: "International conciliation Feb 1941 no 367, YFXC."

If the cataloger had not analyzed this monograph, you would have to find its number from another source (e.g., *CBI*) and look it up in the library catalog under the series *"International Conciliation,* No. 1–   ."

Some institutions issue their own indexes to the monographic series they publish. These are kept on the reference shelves. For instance, the Conference Board, Inc., periodically publishes a *Cumulative Index* to its publications, which lists the publications under subject, author, and title of monograph, and sometimes by series. The card in the catalog looks like the one in Fig. 2.2.

Write on slip words underlined
and class mark–

Churchill, Winston Leonard Spencer, 1874- YFXC

Roosevelt,Franklin Delano *32d. pres. U.S.* 1882
... Address of President Roosevelt, December 29, 1940. President Roosevelt's message to Congress, January 6, 1941. Prime Minister Churchill's address to the Italian people, December 23, 1940. Economic relations between the Americas, by Mordecai Ezekiel... New York city, Carnegie endowment for international peace, Division of intercource and education [1941]

3 p. l., 65–155 p. fold. maps, diagrs. 19½^{cm}. (International conciliation...February, 1941, no.367)
Bibliography:p. 152–155.

1. U.S.–Defenses. 2. American republics. 3. U.S.–Relations (general) with Spanish America. 4. Spanish America–Relations (general) with U.S. I. Churchill, Winston Leonard Spencer, 1874- II.*Ezekiel, Mordecai, 1899-

Library of Congress JX1907.A8 no.367 41-5600
(341.6082) 353.03

Fig. 2.1

M–11
5208

CONFERENCE BOARD, INC.
Reports.
New York. v. 28cm.

CURRENT ISSUES AVAILABLE IN ECONOMICS DIVISION
FULL RECORD OF HOLDINGS IN CENTRAL SERIAL RECORD
Irregular.

1. Business--Per. and soc. publ.--U.S.
NN S 3.72 e OSs CSRs PCs, 1s SLs Es, 1s P(2), 1 (U1s,LC1s,X1s)

Fig. 2.2

The New York Public Library
ASTOR, LENOX AND TILDEN FOUNDATIONS

Call number: M – 11
5208

Author or Periodical: Conference Board

Book Title: Reports no. 527

Date/Vol. No.:

Correct and Legible Name and Address Required

Name _John Smith_

Address _19 Rivermore Rd._

City _Bronx, NY_   Zip _____

School or Business _Fordham Univ._

Seat number: 35

form 28s

Fig. 2.3

After you find the number of the report you want in the *Cumulative Index*, your request slip should look like Fig. 2.3.

Possessive Series
Take care when using the library catalogs to request a monograph series in the correct way. For example, see the catalog entry for a *Farmers' Bulletin* issued by the U.S. Department of Agriculture (Fig. 2.4).

Note that the *Farmers' Bulletin* series and the volume number of this particular *Bulletin* are in parentheses. Although it is not underlined, you would fill out your request slip as shown in Fig. 2.5.

In other cases the cataloger can help you find the correct entry by underlining it, as in the example from the NYPL *Dictionary Catalog, 1911–1971* (Fig. 2.6).

Series within a Series
In the library catalogs you sometimes encounter publications cataloged with two numbered series. The cataloger indicates the more important series, or the chief series, by underlining it on the card, noting the subseries in parentheses.

As in Chapter 1, examples from a specific library are from the New

VPZ

McGrew, T.F.
Turkeys: standard varieties and management. Washington: Gov.Prtg.Off., 1904. 40p. illus. 8°. (United States. Agriculture Dept. Farmers' bull.200.)

1. Turkey.
N.Y.P.L. January 23, 1913.

Fig. 2.4

The New York Public Library
ASTOR, LENOX AND TILDEN FOUNDATIONS
Call number: VPZ

Author or Periodical: United States Agriculture Dept.

Book Title: Farmers' Bulletin # 200

Date/Vol. No.:

Correct and Legible Name and Address Required

Name Mary Jackson
Address 31 Main St.
City NY NY Zip
School or Business Allardyce

Seat number: 72

form 28s

Fig. 2.5

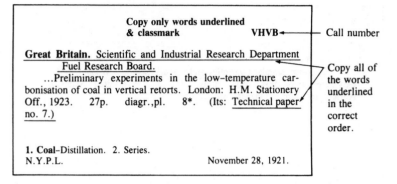

Fig. 2.6

York Public Library. In the following, from the NYPL *Dictionary Catalog, 1911–1971,* we can see two main entries under Espinas, Georges. The first is an author entry, but we are instructed to order the volumes under the monograph series *"Société d'histoire du droit des pays flamands, picards et wallons. Bibliothèque."* The four volumes of the title in the series are numbered 7, 9, 16, and 20. The second card is a series entry—actually a possessive series. The series on the first card is noted on this card as well, but this time the cataloger regards it as the lesser series and reverses its word order (Fig. 2.7a and b).

When you do as the card asks, your request slip is returned and marked "verify." Could the cataloger have underlined the wrong series? You check the catalog under the series "Espinas, Georges. Les Origines de l'association" but you do not find it. You do not find the series "Bibliothèque de la société d'histoire du droit . . ." either. You then check for the series "Société d'histoire du droit . . . ," which you find. You request Espinas's two volumes on the origins of the law of associations as in Fig. 2.8.

You receive the two volumes. You have overcome the cataloger's mistake, and have been reminded how important it is to be alert. Always double-check and think of alternative approaches to your search when you encounter any difficulties.

Indexed Book Sets
Another way of cataloging a monograph series is to "index" or list the monographs below the description of the entry. This practice is

Fig. 2.7a In this case, the series vol. 20 corresponds to fascicule 4 of the title. You request the volumes by series.

Espinas, Georges, 1869-
 ...Les origines du capitalisme...fasc., 1-4. 4. Lille: E.
Raoust, 1933- v. chart; facsims., tables, geneal. table.
25cm. (Societe d'histoire du droit des pays flamands, picards
et wallons. Bibliotheque, Tome, 7,9,16,20)

 Bibliographies included.
 CONTENTS. — [fasc.] 1. Sire Jehan Boinebroke, patricien et drapier douasien. —
[fasc.] 2. Sire Jean de France, patricien et rentier douasien. Sire Jacques le Blond, patricien
et drapier douasien (seconde moitie du XIIIᵉ siecle). — 3. Deux moitie du XIIIᵉ siecle

1. Boinebroke, Jehan,d.ca. 1286. 2. Clothing trade — France — Douai.
3. Capital and labor — France — Douai. 4. Economic history — Flanders.
5. Law, Customary — France — Guines. I. Ser

N.Y.P.L.   September 21, 1934

Espinas, Georges, 1869- ...Les origines du capitalisme... (Card2)
fondations de villes, dans l'artois et la Flandre francaise (Xe–XVe siecles)
Saint-Omer.
Lannoy-du-Nord. —
[fasc.] 4. Le droit economique et social, d'une petite ville artesienne a la fin du
moyen-age, Guines. —

Espinas, Georges, 1860-1948.
 Les origines du droit d'association dans les villes de
l'Artois et de la Flandre francaise jusqu'au debut du XVIᵉ siecle. Lille, E. Raoust,
1941–42 [v.1, 1942]
  2 v. 26 cm. (*His* Les origines de l'association,1) |
  Bibliotheque de la Societe d'histoire du droit des pays flamands, picards et
wallons, 14–15.
  "Bibliographie"; v.1, p. [xxiii-[xxxv]

CONTENTS — 1.t. Histoire — 2. t. Documents.

1. Association and associations — France — Hist. I. Title. Ser (Series:
Bibliotheque de la Societe d'histoire du droit des pays flamands, picards et wallons. 14–15)
I. Societies — France — Artois. 2. Societies, France — Flanders.

New York. Public Libr.   A. 49–1428*
for Library of Congress   (MfCA1)

Fig. 2.7b The first two arrows point to the possessive series indicated wrongly by the cataloger. The third arrow points to the true series.

The New York Public Library Call number: G B WH
ASTOR, LENOX AND TILDEN FOUNDATIONS

Author or Periodical: Societé d'histoire du
Book Title: droit des pays flamands,
picards et wallons
Date/Vol. No.: Bibliothèque t. 14 + 15

Correct and Legible Name and Address Required

Name   Mary Jackson

Address   31 Main St.

City   NY NY   Zip 10007

School or Business   Allardyce Inc

Seat number:

72

form 28s

Fig. 2.8

reserved for a short series of a few volumes, referred to as a *book set.*
The individual title of each volume is listed under the main entry in
order of the volume numbers. A limited series of monographs by different authors, published under one distinctive series title, could be
treated in this way. More common are volumes in a series by one
author, such as those of Randolph Churchill in the example in Fig.
2.9, from the NYPL Research Libraries' *Dictionary Catalog* [1972–
80].

As the ''*R'' indicates, these volumes are on the reference room
shelves. Sometimes secondary source material is elevated to primary
status by the significance of its subject matter. (Similarly two or three

Churchill, Randolph Spencer, 1911-1968. Winston
S. Churchill, by Randolph S. Churchill.
Illustrated with photographs and maps. Boston,
Houghton Mifflin, 1966- -v. illus., ports. 24 cm.
FULL RECORD OF HOLDINGS IN CENTRAL
SERIAL RECORD. Companion vols., containing
documents relating to vol. 2, were completed by Martin
Gilbert. Vol. 3-4 by Martin Gilbert. CONTENTS. - v. 1.
Youth, 1874-1900. - v. 2. Young statesman, 1901-1914. -
Companion v. 2. 1901-1911, pts. 1-2. v. 3. The challenge
of war, 1914-1916. - v. 4. The stricken world, 1916-1922.
NN 73-4229859
[*R-AN (Churchill) 73-3100]

Fig. 2.9

STEWART,ALEXANDER TURNEY,1803–1876

Copy only words underlined
& classmark—
                                                              HAER

RESSEQUE, HARRY E.
    The folklore of A.T. Stewart. (IN: <u>New York folklore</u>
<u>quarterly</u>. Cooperstown.   22cm.   <u>v.18, no. 2 (summer, 1962)</u>
<u>p. 125–141</u>)

    Bibliography, p. 140–141.

1. Stewart, Alexander Turney, 1803–1876.
NN R 8.63 p/j OI (PC)1 (E)1 (LC2, X1)

Fig. 2.10

editions of any encyclopedia are kept on the reference room shelves because significant information in the earlier editions is not found in the latest edition.) In this case, we note that the entry remains open (i.e., "1966– "). We expect more volumes to appear, as the last volume covers Winston Churchill's life only to 1922. On the open reference shelves, a discrete space is left for the continuations.

Catalog Indexing of Magazine Articles

Before the 1960s, when periodical indices had not yet appeared for almost every subject field, librarians indexed magazine articles and essays in books under the author as main entry in the catalog. This is generally not done today.(Fig. 2.10).

On the request slip you write only the title of the periodical, the date, and the call number (Fig. 2.11). But remember to record the pages in your own notes.

Requesting a Work from the Catalog

First you fill out a request slip by printing the name of the author, the title, and the call number. Thus, if you wanted the hypothetical book about James Finance mentioned earlier, you would write:

Jackson, Abel
    Jimmie Finance

The New York Public Library Call number: *HAER*
ASTOR, LENOX AND TILDEN FOUNDATIONS

Author or Periodical: *New York Folklore*

Book Title: *quarterly*

Date/Vol. No.: *V. 18, no. 2. Summer 1962*

Correct and Legible Name and Address Required

Name *John Smith*

Address *19 Rivermore*   Seat number:

City *Bronx NY*   Zip   *35*

School or Business *Fordham U.*

form 28s

Fig. 2.11

and then fill in the call number or classmark from the top righthand corner of the card.

Let us suppose that you want to request a book by Sir Winston Churchill, which you found in the catalog under Churchill's name or under a subject heading (Fig. 2.12 a and b).

You fill out the request slip as follows:

Write down the call number,* the author, and the title as they appear on the card. If there is more than one volume, designate the volume you want, such as "Vol. 2 only," or "all vols" (Fig. 2.13).

How do you request a periodical? Suppose you want the periodical *Finance:* the card in the catalog looks like Fig. 2.14. Thus, you will fill out a request slip that looks like Fig. 2.15 on page 36. Always write the call number, title, and the *month and year* or volume number of a periodical on your request slip.

Let us take another look at the catalog entry for the periodical *Finance* shown in Fig. 2.14. Note that it is marked "v. 72–date; 1957–date." This means that the entry starts with volume 72, published in

---

*Remember that the call number (also called the classmark) is usually given in the top righthand corner of the card of each book and periodical title. This designates where the publication is shelved in the library.

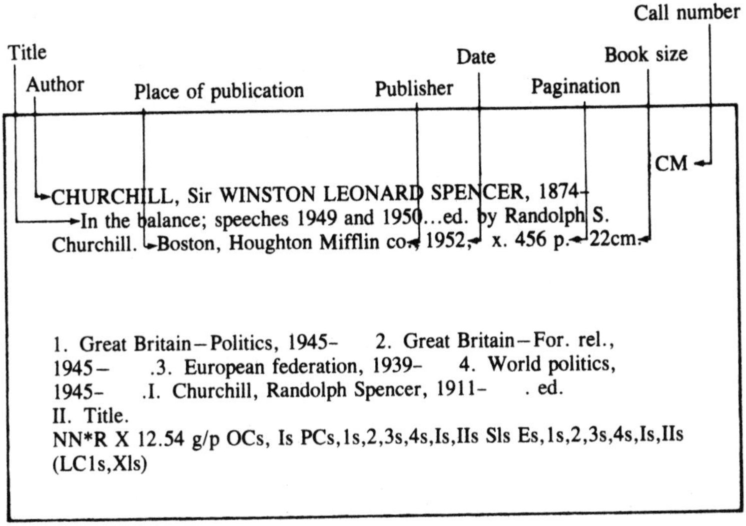

CM

CHURCHILL, Sir WINSTON LEONARD SPENCER, 1874–
In the balance; speeches 1949 and 1950...ed. by Randolph S.
Churchill. Boston, Houghton Mifflin co., 1952. x. 456 p. 22cm.

1. Great Britain–Politics, 1945-   2. Great Britain–For. rel.,
1945–   .3. European federation, 1939-   4. World politics,
1945-   .I. Churchill, Randolph Spencer, 1911-   . ed.
II. Title.
NN*R X 12.54 g/p OCs, Is PCs,1s,2,3s,4s,Is,IIs Sls Es,1s,2,3s,4s,Is,IIs
(LC1s,Xls)

Fig. 2.12a

GREAT BRITAIN--POLITICS, 1945-

CM

CHURCHILL, Sir WINSTON LEONARD SPENCER, 1874–
In the balance-speeches 1949 and 1950...ed. by Randolph S.
Churchill. Boston, Houghton Mifflin co., 1952. x.456 p. 22 cm.

1. Great Britain–Politics, 1945-   .2. Great Britain–For. rel.
1945-   .3. European federation, 1939-   .4. World politics,
1945-   .I. Churchill, Randolph Spencer, 1911-   .ed.
II. Title.
NN*R X 12.54 g/p OCs, Is PCs,1s,2,3s,4s,Is,IIs SLs Es
1s,2,3s,4s,Is,IIs (LC1s,X1s)

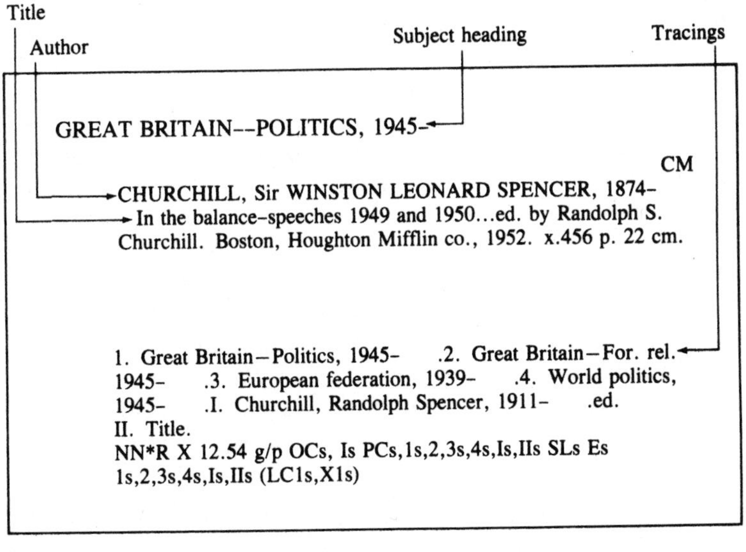

Fig. 2.12b

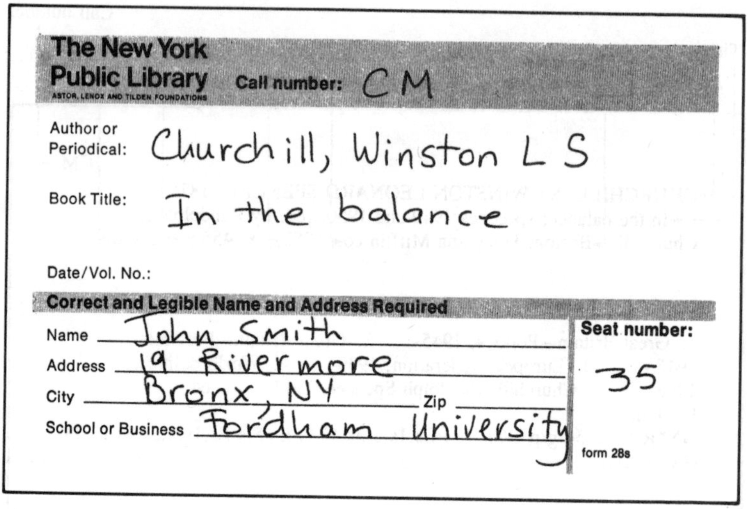

The New York
Public Library   Call number: C M
ASTOR, LENOX AND TILDEN FOUNDATIONS

Author or
Periodical: Churchill, Winston L S

Book Title: In the balance

Date/Vol. No.:

Correct and Legible Name and Address Required

Name ___John Smith_____   Seat number:
Address ___19 Rivermore_____
City ___Bronx, NY_____ Zip _____   35
School or Business ___Fordham University___
                                                    form 28s

Fig. 2.13

1957, and the library contains all subsequent issues to "date," meaning to the present (see below about confirming the "full record"). These issues can be retrieved from the stacks by filling out a request slip in the ordinary way. Issues of the current year, however, as the card informs you, are kept on the current shelves in the Economic and Public Affairs Division (the division's name has been changed since the card was printed); hence, you must ask the librarian of that division for them. For the years before 1957, the card merely informs you of the history of the publication, but it does not say the library has those early titles. Look at the card again. It informs you that the periodical *Finance* began publication in September 1941 under the title *Finance and the Chicago Banker,* which the library did *not* collect (See p. 86 for ways of locating copies). This earlier publication apparently took over the periodical *Chicago Banker,* whose volume numbering it continued; therefore, for issues published before September 1941, you would have to look in the catalog under the *Chicago Banker.* The card also informs you that in August 1942, the *Finance and the Chicago Banker* took over or amalgamated with the *Financial Review,* of which the library has issues published prior to 1942. Last, stamped across the card are the words FULL RECORD OF HOLD-

M-10
1072

FINANCE: all the news of the hire of the dollar. v. 72–
    date: 1957–date
    Chicago, Finance pub. corp.   v.   illus., ports.
    29cm.
        FULL RECORD OF HOLDINGS IN CENTRAL SERIAL RECORD
    CURRENT IN ECONOMICS DIVISION
    Monthly.
    Began publication in Sept. 1941 with title: Finance and the Chicago
banker (not in the library) and until July, 1942, continued the numbering of the
Chicago banker. In Aug., 1942, assumed
                             (Continued)
NN R 7.63 p/jOSs, Is, II PCs, 1s, 2s, II SLs Es, 1s, 2s, II Ps (2s) 1s, 2s,
II (U1s, 1C1s, X1s)

FINANCE: all the news of the hire of the dollar.
        (Cont.)

the v. numbering of another earlier publication, the Financial review.
  One issue each year includes the section: Net worths of the leading
underwriters.

1. Banks and banking--Per. and soc. publ.--U.S. 2. Securities--Per. and
soc. publ.--U.S. I. Finance and the Chicago banker. II. Finance; all the news
of the hire of the dollar. Net worths of the leading underwriters.

Fig. 2.14

INGS IN CENTRAL SERIAL RECORD. This means that the recording of the issues of the periodical *Finance* received by the library are
kept in a central location, which the librarian may telephone or reach
through a computer monitor. Before library procedures were automated, cards recording the years of the periodical (called *holding cards*)
were filed in the catalog behind the main card and kept up to date by
filers. At the NYPL, these holding cards have been removed and the
information on them has been fed into a computer storage terminal, so
that a reference librarian can ascertain the extent of the holdings within
seconds on a computer monitor.

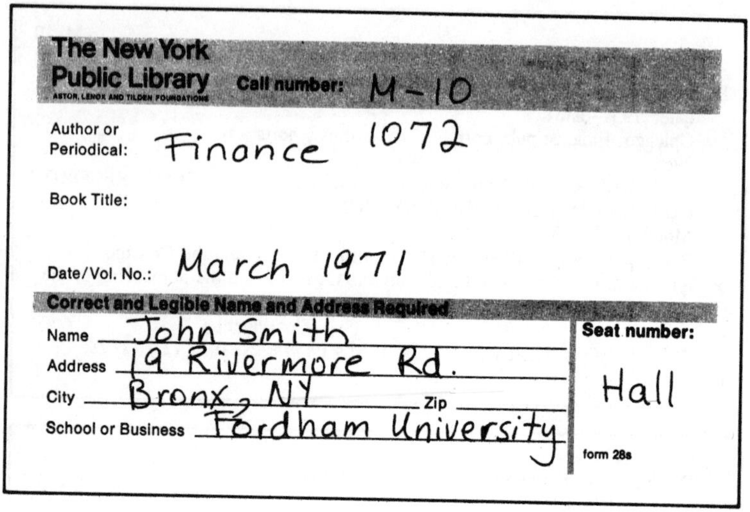

Fig. 2.15

One final point to be made regarding periodical titles: you should know that some periodicals are entered in the catalog by the name of the institution or government agency that issues them—for example, "Ford Foundation. *Newsletter*," or "U.S. Treasury Dept. *Monthly Bulletin*."

If you request a book by a government agency or institution, the agency is listed as the author, thus (Fig. 2.16):

It is logical to state the place first: "Calgary, Alberta," followed by its government agency: "Comptroller." You can fill out the request slip by entering "Calgary, Alberta, Comptroller" as the author, as in (Fig. 2.17).

BOOK CATALOGS

NYPL Dictionary Catalog of the Research Libraries, 1911–71

The *Dictionary Catalog*, (1911–71), bound in black, comprises reproductions of the cards from NYPL's entire main card catalog once shelved in the central catalog room of the General Reference Division (Room

CALGARY, Alberta. Comptroller.
...Financial statistics...and statement of net general
debt and borrowing power.
    FULL RECORD OF HOLDINGS IN CENTRAL SERIAL RECORD
[Calgary, 1926–   21½ cm.

  Annual.
  Title varies slightly.

  1. Finance – Canada – Calgary.

                           PUB. DOC. CAT.

N.Y.P.L.   June 29, 1937

Fig. 2.16

The New York Public Library
ASTOR, LENOX AND TILDEN FOUNDATIONS
Call number: *SYB

Author or Periodical: Calgary, Alberta, Comptroller

Book Title: Financial Statistics

Date/Vol. No.: 1935

Correct and Legible Name and Address Required

Name John Smith
Address 19 Rivermore
City Bronx, NY   Zip
School or Business Fordham University

Seat number: 35

form 28s

Fig. 2.17

315) in 800 black volumes; thus, it catalogs all the books, periodicals, and pamphlets catalogued by the library before 1972, when the card catalog was closed. In 1972 the library began its automated book catalog, and published the NYPL Research Libraries' *Dictionary Catalog,* [1972–1980] in blue binding, the *Supplement,* [1972–1980] in red binding, and the current *Interim List* (green binding). When the card catalog was closed, many shelves of publications for years past were waiting to be cataloged, so you should also consult the computer catalog or look in the later book catalogs (blue, red, and green) for works published before 1972, which are not in the main *Dictionary Catalog, 1911–71.*

NYPL Research Libraries, Dictionary Catalog [1972–1980]

How do you request books and periodicals from the blue and red book catalogs? Following is a sample column from one of the volumes, with comments to help you decipher it.

Let us suppose you are looking for works by Sir Winston Churchill, the British Prime Minister during the Second World War. The first name on the page (Fig. 2.18a) reads "CHURCHILL, WINSTON, 1871–1947." Be careful. This is not the Winston Churchill you want; it is his American cousin. The next name entry is "Churchill, Winston J., 1940– "—the wrong man, again. The third name entry, "Churchill, Winston Leonard Spencer, Sir, 1876–1965," is undoubtedly the man you want. This entry in bold type is called the author entry.

Catalogers try to make an author entry as complete as possible, for the researcher's convenience. For instance, here are the names of Churchills who are authors in the order in which they are listed in the catalog:

Churchill, Randolph Spencer, 1874–
Churchill, Winston, 1871–1947
Churchill, Winston J., 1940–
Churchill, Winston Leonard Spencer, Sir, 1874–1965
Churchill, Winston Spencer, 1940–

In our example, note that the first entry "CHURCHILL, WINSTON, 1871–1947" is in capital letters. This is a subject entry. It heads a list of books about an American novelist, Winston Churchill.

CHURCHILL, WINSTON, 1871-1947.
Barker, Elisabeth. Churchill and Eden at war /.
London , 1978. 346 p. ;   NN 79-4724128 LC
79-314303   **[JFD 79-11149]**

Schneider, Robert W. Novelist to a generation .
Bowling Green, Ohio , c1976. xvi, 333 p. :   NN
76-4895022 LC 76-4643   **[JFE 77-75]**

The scrapbooks of Winston Churchill, American
novelist and politician. [v. p., 1899-1912] 30 v.
NN 79-4633151   **[*Z-2980]**

Churchill, Winston J., 1940- Running in place, by
Winston J. Churchill. New York, G. Braziller
[1973] 218 p. 22 cm. NN 73-4275325 LC
72-92832   **[JFD 73-6526]**

Churchill, Winston Leonard Spencer, Sir, 1874-
1965.
[Works]
The collected works of Sir Winston Churchill.
Centenary limited edition. [London] Library of
Imperial History [1973- -v. maps, ports. 25 cm.
FULL RECORD OF HOLDINGS IN CENTRAL
SERIAL RECORD. Half title: The first collected
works of Sir Winston Churchill. Issued in slipcases.
3000 numbered sets. NYPL set, no. 2052.
CONTENTS. - v. 1. My early life. My African
journey. - v. 2. The story of the Malakand Field
Force. - v. 3. The River War. - v. 4. The Boer war:
London to Ladysmith via Pretoria. Ian Hamilton's
march. - v. 5. Savrola. - v. 6. Lord Randolph
Churchill. - v. 7. Mr. Brodrick's army and other
speeches. - v. 8-12. The world crisis, pt. 1-5. - v. 13.
Thoughts and adventures. - v. 14-15. Marlborough, v.
1-2. - v. 16. Great contemporaries. - v. 17. Arms and
the covenant. - v. 18. Step by step, 1936-1939. - v.
19-21. War speeches, v. 1-3. - v. 22-27. The Second
World War: v. 1 The Gathering storm. - 2. Their
finest hour. - 3. The grand alliance. - v. The hinge of
fate. - 5. Closing the ring. - 6. Triump and tragedy.
Epilogue. - v. 28, 30. Post-war speeches - 1. The
sinews of peace. Europe unite. - 3. Stemming the tide.
The unwritten alliance. - v. 33-34. A history of the
English speaking peoples. [v. 35-38?] Collected essays
of Sir Winston Churchill, v. 1-4: v. 1. Churchill and
War. v. 2. Churchill and politics. v. 3. Churchill and
peole. v. 4 Churchill ar large. NN 74-4958680
[8-*ITG (Gt. Br.: 1974) 74-1241]

Fig. 2.18a

We note that the first main entry, "Barker, Elizabeth," is followed on
the same line by the title *Churchill and Eden at War,* which is a
surprising role for an American novelist. We conclude that the cataloger made a mistake; the entry should come under the subject heading
for Sir Winston Churchill. This is confirmed by inspecting the books,
thus demonstrating the fallibility of book catalogs. This is a useful
lesson for the researcher.

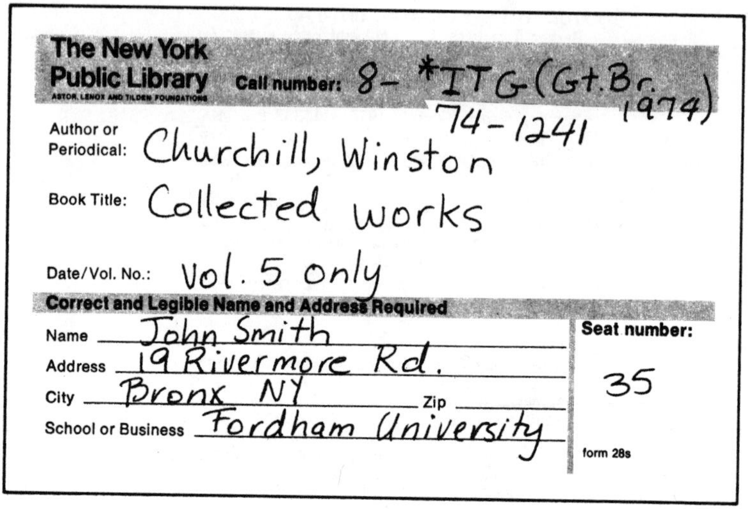
The New York Public Library
ASTOR, LENOX AND TILDEN FOUNDATIONS
Call number: 8- *ITG (Gt.Br. 1974) 74-1241
Author or Periodical: Churchill, Winston
Book Title: Collected works
Date/Vol. No.: Vol. 5 only
Correct and Legible Name and Address Required
Name John Smith
Address 19 Rivermore Rd.
City Bronx NY Zip
School or Business Fordham University
Seat number: 35
form 28s

Fig. 2.18b

The second and third entries under the subject heading appear to be correctly listed under the novelist, Winston Churchill. Note that the third entry is by title, *The scrapbooks* . . . in 30 volumes.

In each case, the call number is in boldface in brackets below and on the right side of the entries (see Fig. 2.18a). (In the card catalog, you will recall, the call number appeared in the upper righthand corner.)

The first entry under "Churchill, Winston Leonard Spencer, Sir," is his *Collected Works*. To get the correct volume, you need to describe it with exactness on your request slip. For instance, if you wish to read Sir Winston Churchill's only novel, *Savrola,* you must write, "Vol. 5 only" (Fig. 2.18b).

You do not need to worry about writing the correct author and title from the NYPL Research Libraries' *Dictionary Catalog,* [1972–1980], because each call number is unique to the book it represents. For instance, in our example (Fig. 2.19a), at the first entry, Churchill is joint author with Franklin Roosevelt (Fig. 2.19a). You may be confused as to the main author entry, Churchill or Roosevelt (Fig. 2.19b). In this case you need write only the call number on the request slip, although it is preferable to fill in the author and short title for verification pur-

(joint author) Roosevelt, Franklin Delano, Pres. U. S., 1882-1945. Roosevelt and Churchill. New York, 1975. xvi, 805 p. NN 75-4584665 LC 74-14854 **[JFE 75-2679]**

Two messages to Poland. [n. p., 1942?] folder ([6] p.) NN 76-4213864 **[*XM-6419]**

Winston S. Churchill: his complete speeches, 1897-1963. Edited by Robert Phodes James. New York, Chelsea House Publishers, 1974. 8 v. (xvi, 8917 p.). illus. 25 cm. NN 74-4703326 **[*R-CM 74-3680]**

Young Winston's wars; the original despatches of Winston S. Churchill, war correspondent, 1897-1900. Edited and with an introd. and notes by Frederick Woods. London, L. Cooper [1972] xxviii, 350 p. ports., maps. 23 cm. NN 73-4295961 **[JFD 73-1499]**

CHURCHILL, WINSTON LEONARD SPENCER, SIR, 1874-1965.
Aigner, Dietrich. Winston Churchill . Göttingen [1975] 152 p., [4] leaves of plates : NN 77-4444118 LC 75-507474 **[JFC 77-1565]**

Fig. 2.19a

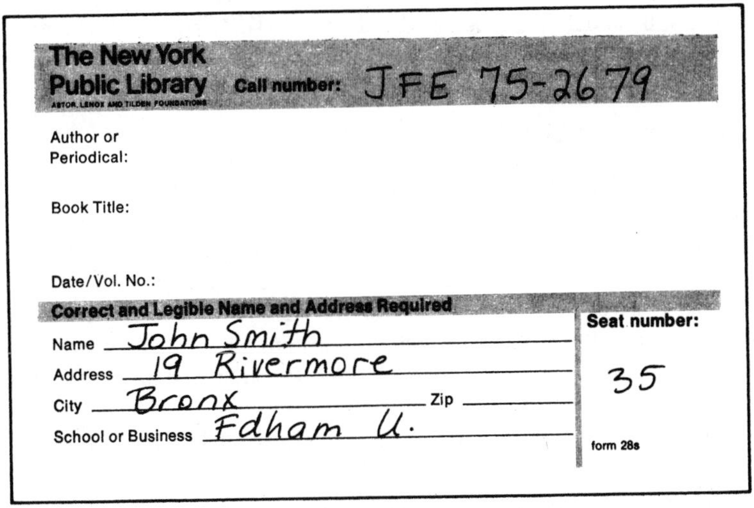
The New York Public Library
ASTOR, LENOX AND TILDEN FOUNDATIONS
Call number: JFE 75-2679

Author or Periodical:

Book Title:

Date/Vol. No.:

Correct and Legible Name and Address Required

Name John Smith

Address 19 Rivermore

City Bronx Zip

School or Business Fdham U.

Seat number: 35

form 28s

Fig. 2.19b

Churchill, Winston Leonard Spencer, Sir, 1874-
        1965.
*Statesmanship : — Carolina Academic Press,
  c1981. viii, 279 p.
        Reg. no.: 0071711
        Call no.: JFE 83-617
Blood, sweat, and tears, — G. P. Putnam's sons
[c1941] x, 462 p. front. (port.)
        Reg. no.: 0059470
        Call no.: JFD 82-2948
The unrelenting struggle; — [1st ed.] — Little,
Brown, 1942. ix, 371 p.
        Reg. no.: 0061181
        Call no.: JFD 82-3547

CHURCHILL, WINSTON LEONARD
    SPENCER, SIR, 1874-1965.
*Callahan, Raymond.
  Churchill : — Scholarly Resources, 1984. xiii, 293
  p.
        Reg. no.: 0190911
        Call no.: JFE 84-2307

*Seldon, Anthony.
  Churchill's Indian summer : — Hodder &
  Stoughton, 1981. xvii, 667 p., [4] leaves of plates :
  ill., ports.
        Reg. no.: 0026240
        Call no.: JFE 82-54

Fig. 2.20

poses (Fig. 2.19b). Remember, you must include author and title of
books from the black retrospective catalogs.

Lower in the column, the catalog lists works about Sir Winston
Churchill under the subject heading "CHURCHILL, WINSTON
LEONARD SPENCER, SIR, 1874–1965."

NYPL Interim List

Following the blue and red book catalogs is a set of volumes called
the NYPL Research Libraries' *Interim List: Index* of publications cataloged after 1981 (green bindings). This catalog is updated every so
often to include new books. Note that each main entry is preceded by
an asterisk (Fig. 2.20). The second entry in the column which is not
asterisked indicates that "Churchill, Winston. . . ." is the author entry and the main entry to a book entitled *Blood, sweat and tears*. The
call number is below the bibliographic description. Further down the
column is the subject heading in capital letters: "CHURCHILL, WIN-
STON LEONARD SPENCER, SIR, 1874–1965." An asterisk indicates that the author entry, "Seldon, Anthony" is the main entry.

Just above the call number for all the entries in these volumes, the

```
0026240
*Seldon, Anthony.
   Churchill's Indian summer : the Conservative
government, 1951-55 / Anthony Seldon. -- London :
Hodder & Stoughton, 1981. xvii, 667 p., [4] leaves
of plates : ill., ports. ; 24 cm.
   Bibliography: p. 627-645.
   Includes index.
   LCCN:  81181385
   1. Great Britain -- Politics and government --
1945-1964. 2. Churchill, Winston Leonard Spencer,
-- Sir, -- 1874-1965.
         Call no.: [JFE 82-54]
```

Fig. 2.21

term "Reg. no." appears, for registration number. This number refers to an entry in a set of volumes called *Interim List: Register,* which accompanies the *Interim List: Index* volumes. Every entry has a registration number. These registration numbers are listed numerically in the *Register* volumes. For instance, the registration number for the book by Seldon is 0026240. Turning to the number in the *Register,* you find that the entry is given a fully bibliographic citation including tracings (Fig. 2.21).

Some libraries have the *Register* on microfilm and the *Index* in book form.

The computer catalog known as the Carlyle System uses this *Index* and *Register* format. You can call to the screen the *Index* citation of a publication to get its call number. If you want the full bibliographic citation and the subject-heading tracings, you can call its *Register* to the screen. The NYPL catalogs its recent acquisitions on the Carlyle computer program. You, as a reader, simply type out instructions and a monitor displays the call number and a description of the publication you want.

Carlyle System

The Carlyle System is a simplified online system limited to the collection of the research library in which it is located, for use by the reader. The NYPL's Carlyle System, called CATNYP, supplements the printed catalogs. Commands such as f/s (find subject), f/a (find author), f/t (find title) are designed to display for the reader a brief citation and the callnumber. Find author and title (f/a and t) narrows the field response. If you are unsure of the exact title, you may type the request f keyword Portrait artist young man. For example, suppose you remember only the last name of the author of the book you wish to request (Armstrong):

Type: f/a Armstrong (press return key; after every command, press return key).
Items found: 36
Type: display (or d) 1–5.

You review the items displayed and find that item 5 is the book you want:

5. Armstrong, Lillian. Renaissance miniature painters and classical imagery: the master of the Putti and his Venetian workshop/Lillian Armstrong.
London: Harvey Miller, 1981 JFF 83–126.

This is the *normal* display.

If you request the brief citation, type display brief 5 (or db5) and the part of the citation after the word workshop is eliminated. If you request a full citation (d full 5) to be printed (Print full 5), it will look like this (Fig. 2.22):

```
Search request:    F  A  ARMSTRONG
Items found:       36
Print request:     PRINT FULL 5

Item 5.

AUTHOR          Armstrong, Lilian.
TITLE           Renaissance miniature painters & classical imagery: the
                Master of the Putti and his Venetian workshop / Lilian
                Armstrong.
PUBLICATION     London: Harvey Miller, c1981.
DESCRIPTION     viii, 223 p., [5] leaves of plates: ill. (some col.)
                facsims.; 28 cm.
NOTES           Includes indexes.
                Bibliography; p. 139-148.
SUBJECTS        1. Master of the Putti, 15th cent. 2. Master of the London
                Pliny, 15th cent. 3. Illumination of books and manuscripts,
                Renaissance--Italy--Venice.

CALL NUMBER  JFF 83-126
```

Fig. 2.22

Two important commands are the modifying command and the backup command. *Modifying commands* are the words *AND, OR,* and *AND NOT,* followed by the type of search (such as author, title, or subject) and then the words that modify your original request. For example:

AND title information processing
OR subject solar
AND NOT subject environment

AND narrows your search to items that contain both the words in your original search and the words after the modifying command. OR expands or enlarges your search to include items containing either the words in your original request or those after the modifying command. AND NOT includes items containing the words in your original request, but not the words after the modifying command.

For example:

Type: f/a joseph conrad
Items found: 27
Modifying command: AND t Victory
Items found: 0
Backup command: BACKUP
Items found: 27

The backup command returns to your previous request after your modifying command or a Find command have produced a new search result. To see the results of previous unmodified searches directly, use the command BACKUP FIND. You can return to previous searches with the command BACKUP FIND after completing two or more searches; it can be used up to five times in succession:

Type: f/t Mexico and not new and not mayan
Items found: 64
    f/s indians and not mayan and not mexican
Items found: 249
    f/s anthropology and mexico and not new
Items found: 5
BACKUP FIND
Items found: 249
BACKUP FIND
Items found: 64

If you find that your request calls up a large number of items that you wish to scan, type d b (for display brief), to allow more items to fit on the screen. But, if possible, try to narrow the possibilities by more specific search commands. If you see an item for which you wish the call number, type d normal (for display normal). To see its subject headings, type d full (for display full). After scanning many items, if you wish to return to an earlier item, type, for example, d1 or d5 to return to item 1 or 5.

Research Libraries Information Network (RLIN)

RLIN is a computerized acquisition, cataloging, and searching service in which many research libraries throughout the United States, including NYPL, cooperate. You can bring an item up on the screen of the RLIN terminal by typing instructions to the computer. Since RLIN was set up by the Research Libraries Group (RLG), whose purpose is to share the acquiring of books by subject fields among its member libraries and to facilitate interlibrary loan, we explain how to use the terminal in detail in the section on interlibrary loan. You may have to use RLIN, however, to find publications cataloged in the library that are too recent to be included in the NYPL *Interim List*.

You type "fin" for "find," "pn" for "personal name," and "tp" for "title phrase." Typing "fin pn carter, j and tp presidential papers" should bring to the screen the complete bibliographic citation with symbols for the libraries that hold the publication. If you see "NYPG" you know that the New York Public Library has it. To find the call number, so that you can request it from the stacks, you type "par" for "partial" and the citation appears in the form in which the library catalogued it with the NYPL call number;

Different Cataloging Arrangements

To this point we have been talking about Dictionary Catalogs in which entries are filed alphabetically.

Some libraries use the Divided Catalog. Cards for authors and titles are arranged alphabetically in one list and subject cards are listed in a separate alphabetical arrangement. There are variations on this theme— authors may be separated from titles to form a third catalog, for instance, or works about individuals may be filed with authors' names in a Names catalog (as in the NYPL Branch Libraries Catalogs).

The Classified Catalog arranges works in a logical subject order, placing similar books together, under a numbering system. The Engineering Society's Library in New York City requires you to locate the classification number for a particular subject before you can use the subject card catalog.

The Dewey Decimal Classification System arranges books by subject number. In the circulating libraries it is used to make it easier for the public to locate books on the open shelves; in the case of research libraries, the public uses either a Dictionary or Divided Catalog to look up the classification number. Similarly the U.S. Library of Congress uses a subject numbering classification, but its readers use a Dictionary Catalog to look up the L.C. call number.

Catalogs in Other Research Libraries

The library of the British Museum in London uses large leather-backed volumes into which are inserted pages with pasted-on printed bibliographic descriptions of its holdings, with call numbers. These insertions are arranged alphabetically by name.

To find books by subject heading you use bound printed volumes for the early periods and microfilm cassettes for after 1970 (see p. 142).

The Bibliothèque Nationale in Paris records its holdings in a variety of catalog forms over the years: first, in printed book catalogs, then card catalogs, then small looseleaf or sheaf catalogs, then card catalogs again. Periodicals are cataloged in a separate card catalog. These catalogs are designated by the years of acquisition they cover. Remember, however, that a book published in 1890 may have been acquired by the library in 1950 and will be located through the catalog covering acquisitions in 1950. We discuss the catalogs of the Bibliothèque Nationale on p. 144.

OPEN-SHELF REFERENCE BOOKS

How do you request books you cannot find in the library catalogs?

If you know only the title, you will not find the book in the NYPL *Dictionary Catalog* unless the title was considered distinctive. Titles of directories, encyclopedias, and collected readings are considered distinctive and given main entries in preference to their editors or compilers. A book by the famous Sir Winston Churchill, *In the Balance,* was considered to have a distinctive title and given a title added entry. But ordinary books are listed in the catalog only by the author's names; if you can remember only a title, you should consult other sources to find the author's name. Suppose, for instance, you want to see a novel entitled *Leave Her to Heaven,* and you have forgotten the name of the author; you would proceed to consult the following:

Books in Print (BIP) lists all books currently available from American publishers. Author, title, and subject indexes are published annually. Look in the title index volume of BIP for *Leave Her to Heaven* to find the author. Monthly indexes of books in print, entitled *Forthcoming Books,* announce recently published or about-to-be-published books. *Whittaker's Books of the Month to Come* announces publications in England. If the book you want is not listed in the BIP you may check *Canadian Books in Print* and *British Books in Print.*

You cannot find *Leave Her to Heaven* in BIP, because it is out of print. What do you do next? You turn to a valuable comprehensive source, *The Cumulative Book Index* (CBI), which is a monthly publication listing all books and pamphlets in the English language by author, title, series, and subject heading. It is cumulated quarterly, annually, and every few years. If you have a rough idea of the date of the work, work systematically through volumes covering the period, quickly checking under title. You locate *Leave Her to Heaven* in the CBI volume covering 1943–1948 and note its author, Ben Ames Williams. Then you can locate the library classmark for the novel by looking in the library catalog under Williams, Ben Ames.

If you know only the title of a book in a foreign language, you can find the author in the national bibliography published by the foreign country.*

How do you request articles in periodicals, newspapers, and books? Let us suppose you need to research a bibliography of sources such as the following:

1. Letelier, Isabel and Michael Moffit, "Supporting repression: multinational banks in Chile." *Race and Class* 20: 111–28, Autumn 1978. In this case you look for the periodical *Race and Class* in the library catalog and fill out a request slip with the call number of the periodical, the title of the periodical, and the date of the article only.

2. Jahn, G. R., "Image of the railroad in Anna Karenina." *Slavic*

*For the titles of national bibliographies, see, Vladimir M. Palic, *Government Publications: A Guide to Bibliographic Tools,* 4th ed. (Washington, D.C.: Library of Congress, 1975).

and East European Journal 25: 1–10. Summer 1981. You would use the same procedure as described.

3. Vicker, Roy. "In the middle: Cairo, as big recipient of aid, heeds views of both U.S., Saudis . . ." *Wall St. Journal* 193:1 + March 7, 1979. In this case you request *The Wall St. Journal* for March 7, 1979 (which is on microfilm) and look for the article on page 1.

4. Simons, Henry C. "Unions as Monopolies." In C. Lowell Harriss. *Selected Readings in Economics* (Englewood Cliffs, N.J.:Prentice-Hall, 1958), pp. 195–200. In this case you look in the library catalog under "Harriss, C. Lowell, ed," for the book *Selected Readings* and request it by call number.

How do you find articles on a given subject?

You look in periodical indices, most of which are issued every two weeks, and cumulated quarterly and annually. There are periodical indices for almost all subject fields. The most popular are *The Readers' Guide to Periodical Literature* (which indexes articles by author and subject), the Public Affairs Information Service (PAIS) *Bulletin*, the *Applied Science and Technology Index,* and the *Bibliography Index.*

After finding an article in the periodical index, you proceed to find the call number for the periodical in which the article was printed.

For example, suppose you have been given citation 2 in the preceding bibliography but could remember only that it concerned Tolstoi's novel *Anna Karenina* and was printed in 1981. You would look in the *Humanities Index* for 1981 under Tolstoi and find the following:

TOLSTOI, Lev Nikolaevich, graf

about

Image of the railroad in Anna Karenina, G. R. Jahn

Slavic & E Eur 25: 1–10. Summ '81

You find the full title of the journal in a list of abbreviations in the front of the index volume and then check the library catalog for that journal's call number.*

---

*Research libraries catalog the first volume of serials they receive, and leave the entry open to indicate that succeeding volumes will be placed on the shelf after the first volume. Therefore, to find the call number, look in the library catalog that covers the year the first volume was issued.

Suppose you have been given the author and subject of a pamphlet, but you cannot find it listed in the library catalogs. What do you do?

You look in *The Cumulative Book Index* (if it is in the English language). For example, you have been told to read a book by David Price on the instability in the Near East, but you do not know that it is a numbered monograph in a monograph series (monograph means book), and moreover the library has not analyzed this series (see the description of "analyzed series" on p. 24). To add to your problems, you cannot find a book on that subject under the author in the library catalog, although you know it was published in 1976. When you consult *The Cumulative Book Index* for 1977, you might come across something near your subject area under the entry "Price, David Lynn, Oil and Middle East Security. (Georgetown Univ., Center for Strategic and Int. Studies. Washington Papers v.41 no. 43) 84p. $3. Sage Publications." When you look in the library catalog for "Washington Papers" you find the entry "Washington Papers, no. 1–   ; 1972–   ," with the call number. You then request "Washington Papers, No. 43 only."

You can also find the same bibliographic information in the Public Affairs Information Service *Bulletin* for 1977 under the subject heading Petroleum Industry and the subheading Near East.

If the monograph were in a European language other than English, you could probably find its monograph series and its number under the same subject headings in the Public Affairs Information Service *Foreign Language Index.*

THE REQUEST SLIP

You know how to get to the correct department in a research library, use the reference books on the reference shelves, use the catalogs, use the periodical indices, and request books, pamphlets, and periodicals from the stacks. All of these steps are elementary to doing research. After requesting a book from the stacks, however, instead of receiving the book, you may receive your request slip back. In this case, look at the listing of "reports" on the slip. Some libraries list these on the reverse side of the slip, others at the bottom of the slip. In the New York Public Library, for example, the reports are listed on the reverse side, like this (Fig. 2.23):

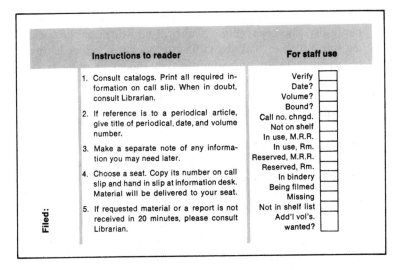

Instructions to reader	For staff use
1. Consult catalogs. Print all required information on call slip. When in doubt, consult Librarian.	Verify □
	Date? □
	Volume? □
	Bound? □
2. If reference is to a periodical article, give title of periodical, date, and volume number.	Call no. chngd. □
	Not on shelf □
	In use, M.R.R. □
3. Make a separate note of any information you may need later.	In use, Rm. □
	Reserved, M.R.R. □
	Reserved, Rm. □
4. Choose a seat. Copy its number on call slip and hand in slip at information desk. Material will be delivered to your seat.	In bindery □
	Being filmed □
	Missing □
5. If requested material or a report is not received in 20 minutes, please consult Librarian.	Not in shelf list □
	Add'l vol's. wanted? □

Filed:

Fig. 2.23

1. "Verify." This means you should take the catalog drawer or the book catalog with your returned slip to a librarian for verification. You may have made a mistake when copying the catalog entry. If your request was for a periodical, the librarian needs to check to see if the issue you requested is in the library. It may be in the bindery or on the current shelves.

2. "Call no. changed" means that a publication found in the card catalog has been recataloged in a newer book catalog and given a different call number.

3. "Not on shelf" simply means that the book cannot be found on the shelf where it should be. It could be misshelved, or in use (although no slip is on file for it), or lost (although not officially declared lost). You may request a "Search and Notify," which means the staff searches for the book and notifies you by postcard if it is located.

4. "In use, M.R.R." means that the book is being read at that moment in the Main Reading Room. "In use, Rm–" with the room number indicated means that the book is being read in one of the departments. Try requesting the book in a few days.

5. "Reserved" means that the book is on the reserve shelves in the

Main Reading Room or in one of the departments. The name of
the reader who reserved the book will be written on the back of
the slip, which enables you to find the book reserved under his or
her name, and take it for your use. You should return the book to
the reserve shelves; otherwise it will be returned to the stacks.

6. "In bindery" means that the book or periodical is being bound
   and will not be reshelved perhaps for months.
7. "Being filmed." If the book is actually in the process of being
   filmed, you cannot retrieve it. But it may be either waiting to be
   filmed or filmed but not cataloged, in which cases the librarian
   can retrieve it from the filming room for you.
8. "Missing." This means stolen. Look again in the catalogs to see
   if the book has been replaced and given a different call number,
   or if there are earlier or newer editions.
9. "Not in shelf list." The shelf list catalog contains cards for every
   book and periodical title cataloged in the library. The cards are
   filed by call number. When the library page cannot find the book
   you requested, he or she checks the shelf catalog to see if the call
   number is correct. If you receive the report that the book is not
   in the shelf list catalog, the call number is incorrect.
10. "Add'l vols., wanted?" means that there are many volumes per
    year of the series you have requested and the library page has sent
    up some volumes and wants to know if you want additional vol-
    umes.
11. "On loan" means that the book you want is out on loan under
    the library's interlibrary loan system.

The reverse side of the slip for the library of the British Museum
directs the reader to special areas where the book is shelved when it
cannot be found in the stacks. (In some libraries, such as the NYPL,
the librarians check request slips when you present them and direct
you to the correct area before you file them).

On the request slip for the British Library reproduced in Fig. 2.24
the box for checking the catalog entry is crossed through and the words
"the entry" have been crossed out and replaced by the word "dates."
The order is for a serial, and you are being requested to check under
the main entry (where the dates of the full run of the serial is given)
to make sure the library has the dates you requested. The library page
can find no issue earlier than 1960.

REASON FOR NON-DELIVERY

In use. If urgently required apply to:

☐ Reading Room Centre Desk
☐ North Library Issue Counter
☐ Official Publications Issue Desk
☐ North Library Gallery Issue Desk
Name _____ date _____

☐ At Binders   Order No _____
☐ At Labellers   Bindery _____
☐ At Furbishers   Date _____
If urgently required apply to The Superintendent, Book Delivery Services, Reading Room

It is regretted that:

☐ this work was destroyed by bombing in the war, we have not been able to acquire a replacement
☐ this work has been mislaid
☐ this work has been missing since
_____

This work is on the reference shelves of:

☐ The Reading Room   ☐ The North Library
☐ The North Library Gallery ☐ The Map Library
☐ The Official Publications Library
☐ Music Reading Area
☐ The last number of the series on the shelf at this shelf-mark is _____

☐ Please give volume number required
   DATES
☒ Please check ~~the entry~~ in the General Catalogue again and if necessary show the entry to the Enquiry Desk staff
☐ This work has been transferred to the Science Reference Library.
☐ This work is at present in the Reprographic Section and is temporarily unavailable
   Reprographic No _____ date _____
☐ For Further information please apply to Book Delivery Enquiries, or Enquiry Desk

PB SD84   *First on shelf 1960*

Fig. 2.24

For requesting publications at the Bibliothèque Nationale in Paris, there are two request forms or slips—one for books and the other for periodicals. The slip shown in Fig. 2.25, you will notice, indicates where an error was made. In this case, the library page has returned the slip with the error circled in red pencil and a check mark in the appropriate box.

SUPPLEMENTARY CATALOGS

Authority Catalogs

For every card in the public catalog there is a duplicate card in the authority catalogs, which are kept in the cataloging rooms. If you suspect a book should be in the research library but cannot find it in the public catalog, you should ask the librarian to check the authority catalog.

There are three authority catalogs: the authority name catalog, the authority serial catalog, and the authority government publications cat-

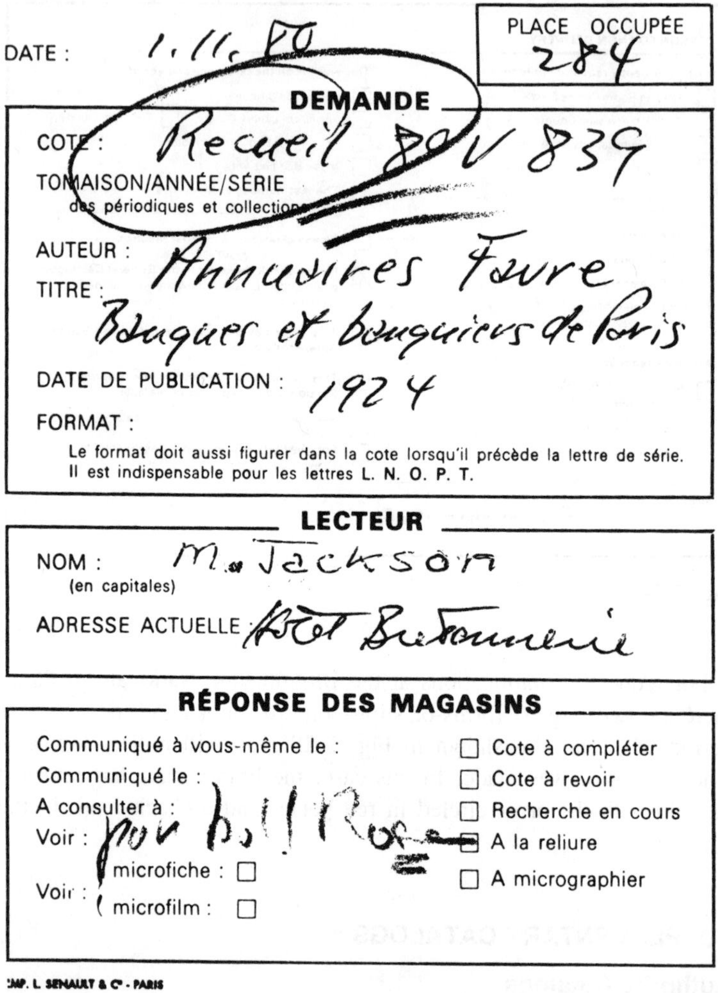
DATE : 1.11.80

PLACE OCCUPÉE 284

DEMANDE

COTE : Recueil 8° V 839

TOMAISON/ANNÉE/SÉRIE
des périodiques et collections

AUTEUR : Annuaires Faure

TITRE : Banques et banquiers de Paris

DATE DE PUBLICATION : 1924

FORMAT :

Le format doit aussi figurer dans la cote lorsqu'il précède la lettre de série.
Il est indispensable pour les lettres L. N. O. P. T.

LECTEUR

NOM : M. Jackson
(en capitales)

ADRESSE ACTUELLE : Hôtel Britannia

RÉPONSE DES MAGASINS

Communiqué à vous-même le :
Communiqué le :
A consulter à :
Voir :
Voir : microfiche : ☐ microfilm : ☐

☐ Cote à compléter
☐ Cote à revoir
☐ Recherche en cours
☐ A la reliure
☐ A micrographier

IMP. L. SENAULT & Cie - PARIS

Fig. 2.25

alog. The authority card establishes the correct form for that entry. In the case of Sir Winston Churchill, for instance, it refers to biographies establishing the correct form of his name, or change of name, and his birth and death dates. In the case of corporate entries, the authority card establishes the correct form for the catalog entry, notes the background of the corporate body, its name changes, and the dates of those changes. It refers to authoritative sources for the form of entry and gives cross-references from other forms.

Deferred Catalogs

When books that by all reasoning should be in the research library are found neither in the public catalog nor in the authority catalog, ask the librarian to check the deferred catalogs. Many shelves of publications are deferred for future cataloging. Deferred publications are often from foreign publishers and frequently are government publications. You can request a deferred publication by its deferred number. In recent years research libraries, lacking funds for cataloging, have deferred tens of thousands of books, including new books from standard publishers. You must ask the librarian to retrieve those publications. *This point cannot be emphasized enough.*

Special Catalogs

Special catalogs may be in card or book form. They cover the collections in specific subject areas. Often special catalogs remain the only guide to their collections. This is generally true of manuscript collections for which the catalog may be found only in the manuscripts room. Special collections of rare books and manuscripts such as the NYPL's Berg Collection and Arents Collections maintain catalogs peculiar to their collections alone.

In recent years many of these special supplementary catalogs have been reproduced in book form. Following is a list of such book catalogs that record the basic collections of NYPL's special or subject collections.

NYPL *Dictionary Catalog:*
  of Art and Architecture
  of the Dance Collection
  of the Henry W. and Albert A. Berg Collection of English and
    American Literature
  of the History of the Americas Collection
  of the Manuscript Division

of the Map Division
of the Music Collection
of the Prints Division
of the Oriental Collection
of the Rare Book Division
of the Rodgers and Hammerstein Archives
of the Schomburg Collection of Negro Literature and History
of the Theatre and Drama Collections
of the Slavonic Collection
and Shelf List of the Spencer Collection of Illustrated Books and
    Manuscripts and Fine Bindings
NYPL. The Imprint Catalog in the Rare Book Division
NYPL. Rare Book Division. Catalog of Special and Private Presses
    in the Rare Book Division

When researching a subject that is likely to be supplemented by specialized cataloging treatment, such as music scores, photographic collections, or oral history, keep a lookout for catalogs in book form of
other libraries. Here are a couple of examples:

France. Fondation Nationale des Sciences Politiques, Paris. Centre de
    documentation contemporaine. *Index* (Bibliographie courante d'ar-
    ticles des periodiques postèrieurs à 1944 sur les problèmes poli-
    tiques, economiques et sociales (1948) v. 1–17.

Premier supplement (1969) v. 1
Deuxième supplement (1970) v. 1
Troisième supplement (1971) v. 1
Quatrième supplement (1972) v. 1
Cinquième supplement (1973) v. 1
Sixième supplement (1974) v. 1–2
Septième supplement (1974) v. 1–2
Huitième supplement (1975) v. 1–2
Neuvième supplement (1976) v. 1–2
Dixième supplement (1977) v. 1
Onzième supplement (1978) v. 1–2
From 1983 on, this index is found only in data-base form: ESOP.

Newberry Library, Chicago, Edward E. Ayer Collection. *Dictionary Catalog of Americana and American Indians in the Newberry*

Library, 16 vols. 1961. First Supp. 3 vols., 1970. Second Supp. 4 vols., 1980.

For a listing of other similar catalogs, see the following reference:

Bonnie R. Nelson. *A Guide to Published Library Catalogs* (Metchuen, NJ; London; Scarecrow, 1982). ''The proper use of this wide range reference book puts the world's written records into our hands.'' It lists and describes major catalogs of significant collections, generally multivolume, published since 1960 (excluding the printed book catalogs of the nineteenth and early twentieth centuries). It represents entire collections from the earliest acquisitions to recent years.

Book catalogs like those issued by the British Library and the Library of the London School of Economics are printed catalogs. Printed book catalogs can cover the holdings of many libraries and are used to locate books for interlibrary loan. An example is the *National Union Catalog* (NUC), a multivolume set that lists books and pamphlets printed before 1956. The entries are by author and given the symbols for the research libraries in North America from which the book may be borrowed by your research library at your request. After 1956 decennial, quinquennial, and annual volumes follow, up to the present.

Its counterpart for serials is the *Union List of Serials* and its supplements.

NYPL Catalog of Government Publications in The Research Libraries

A card catalog reproduced in book form, the NYPL *Catalog of Government Publications in The Research Libraries* shows the Library's holdings in government publications before 1972. There was a large cataloging backlog when this catalog was closed, therefore, some government publications issued before 1972, particularly congressional hearings, are found in the NYPL Research Libraries' *Dictionary Catalog* [1972–1980].

The idea of the Government Publications Catalog was to separate government documents from the rest of the collection in the catalog, to make them easier to find. The catalog is arranged alphabetically by government entity of the publishing body: country, province, county, city or town. Within this entity, the entries are arranged alphabetically by government agency, which is listed in inverted form (e.g., Agriculture, Department of). Within the agency, government serials are arranged in alphabetical order before the monographs, which are arranged chronologically by date of publication. Because government publications are recognized most easily by government body and date of publication, you can see the value of this catalog.

Supplementary Catalogs: Publications in Microform

Under the rubrick of supplementary catalogs we refer to catalogs that serve as the library catalog because the publications listed in them can be found only in these sources, using the entry numbers in them in lieu of call numbers. Most prominent of these is the *Monthly Catalog of United States Government Publications,* which since the 1950s has provided direct access to the publications listed in it on microprint card. Since the early 1980s when the U.S. government began publishing in microfiche, the *Monthly Catalog* has provided access by Superintendent of Documents number to those government publications issued in microfiche. You must use this number as a call number. The NYPL does not enter such publications in the library catalogs. The use of the *Monthly Catalog* is described in the section on government publications.

A Checklist of Official Publications of the State of New York, a monthly, serves the same purpose. It provides the call numbers to state publications, all of which have been reproduced in microform, since 1975.

Economic Working Papers Bibliography, an annual listing of working papers in economics issued from institutions around the world, serves as the catalog for the publications it lists, all of which are on microfiche.

Several of these kinds of catalogs exist, and you can expect more. Some have adopted the approach of the Congressional Information Service (CIS) *Index to U.S. Government Publications,* in which you find the item you wish in the detailed *Index* volume, which leads you to an abstract of the publication in the companion *Abstract* volume. Here you find a number opposite the entry that serves as a call number to the publication on microfiche located in the microform reading room of the library.

Publications on Microfilm

The library has recataloged some publications listed in the retrospective catalogs because it put the publications onto microfilm or microfiche and discarded the paper volumes. The recataloged item appears in the newer catalogs with its changed call number. If the publication is on microfilm, the call number begins with ''*Z − .'' If it was put on microfiche, the call number begins with ''*X − .'' When you encounter these call numbers, you proceed to the microform reading areas to read the publication.

Some departments maintain separate lists of periodicals on microfilm that were recataloged with film call numbers.

3

Tools of Research

No longer a novice, my dear Watson.

Feel free to skip through this section and read only what interests you. But before you plunge into the more sophisticated library tools, please be sure you are well practiced in the elementaries. And always remember a basic term, *main entry*. The ALA defines it as "A full catalog entry, usually the author entry, giving all the information necessary to the complete identification of a work. In a card catalog this entry bears also the tracing of all other headings under which the work in question is entered in the catalog."

The last sentence refers to arabic numbered subject headings and the Roman numeraled added author and title entries, as seen at the foot of the card in Fig. 2.12b. They also appear above the main entry on cards filed in the catalog, to help you find the main entry. By using the subject tracings at the foot of a main entry card, you can find books in the catalog under those subject headings relevant to the subject you are researching. The Library stopped listing tracings in the NYPL Research Libraries, *Dictionary Catalog* [1972–1980] but resumed them in the *Interim List*.

It is the main entry that you write opposite the author designation on your request slip, followed by the title of the book. It is important to remember, when requesting a periodical, that the title is usually the main entry.

Let us suppose that the library catalogs and periodical indices fail to lead you to the information you want. You need more sophisticated means to gain access to publications in the collection. General guides to reference works lead you to specific sources for the subject you are researching. The most widely consulted are Winchell's *Guide to Reference Sources* and the later revision Sheehy's *Guide to Reference*

Books. In the following pages you will find a few of the most-used titles as examples of standard reference works. They are briefly cited to serve as aids to your research—full bibliographic information, when needed, may be found in the general reference guides or the library catalogs.

These sources are characterized by the format by which they give you access to the collection. Each one of these formats or library tools is further characterized by the broad subject division in which it is primarily used.

THE BIBLIOGRAPHY: ITS FORMS AND USES

Bibliography (ALA definition [in part]) A list of books, maps, etc., differing from a catalog in not being necessarily a list of materials in a collection, a library, or a group of libraries.

The book bibliography concentrates on subjects in depth, sometimes to the extent of being an art form.

You may find book bibliographies through *bibliographies of bibliographies,* which arrange bibliographies by subject, by time period, or by geographical area. For example, a list of bibliographies of the literary works of English authors of the twentieth century is a bibliography of bibliographies by subject. Here are examples found in the open reference shelves in General Research:

Index bibliographicus: v.1, Science and Technology, v.2, Social Sciences; v. 3, Humanities; v.4, General Bibliography.

A World Bibliography of Bibliographies and of Bibliographical Catalogues, Calendars, Abstracts, Digests and the Like. 5 vols.

Internationale Personal Bibliographies, 1800–1959 (This indexes bibliographies contained in books, periodicals, biographical dictionaries, academic annuals, Festschriften, and other sources. The first edition should be consulted for many names that were dropped from the second for political reasons.)

You may also find bibliographies by catalog subject heading. The letters ''BIBL.'' following the subject heading indicate a bibliography (Fig. 3.1).

This reproduction from the card catalog illustrates the case in point.

CHURCHILL, SIR WINSTON LEONARD SPENCER, 1874 – 1965
--BIBL.   D – 14
                                                                    9850
WOODS, FREDERICK.
   A bibliography of the works of Sir Winston Churchill.
[Toronto] University of Toronto press, 1963.   340 p.
illus., ports.   22cm.

1. Churchill, Sir Winston Leonard Spencer, 1874- --Bibl.
NN R 3.64 e/B OC PC,1 SL E, 1   (LC1,X1)

Fig. 3.1

You can see that Churchill wrote a great deal throughout his long life
because this book contains 340 pages.

Bibliographies to Books

Often bibliographies are arranged to indicate the importance of each
source and its contribution to the subject. In this vein, descriptive and
textual bibliographies place an artist's works in chronological sequence and indicate when changes took place in the author's view-
point, which is helpful to a biographer.

   To remain comprehensive, some book bibliographies are updated
periodically to include the latest works on the subject. Some periodicals, for instance, devote one issue a year to listing new publications
in the subject fields they cover.

   As the preceding example of the bibliography to Churchill's works
(Fig. 3.1) illustrates, you can sometimes locate bibliographies to particular subjects without going through bibliographies to bibliographies.
Aside from using the library catalog, you can use bibliographies to
books such as the following:

*MLA International Bibliography of Books and Articles on the Modern
   Languages and Literatures,* 1921-   Annual. Since 1969 this has
   been divided into three sections, each with a separate table of con-

tents, list of journal title abbreviations, and index of critics. I. General literature and English, American, Celtic, and Medieval and neo-Latin literatures, and folklore. (Australian, Canadian, Caribbean, and other English-language literatures of the world are in the opening division of the English literature section.) II. European, Asian, African, and Latin American literatures. III. General linguistics and studies of specific languages. (This reference is designed to serve the needs of those researching in a theme, idea, literary form, or similar topic.)

American Book Publishing Record (a cumulation of American book production for the years 1876–1949 in 15 vols.).

American Book Publishing Record Cumulative, 1956–77, in 15 vols.

Index Translationum. International bibliography of translations, 1932– .

Cumulative Book Index (for publications in English), with which you already are familiar, is a bibliography to books, broadly speaking.

Biblio (for publications in French) *catalogue des ouvrages parus en langue française dans le monde entier,* 1934–70 (annual); and *Les Livres de l' année, Biblio,* 1971– .

Deutsches Bucherverzeichnis (for publications in German), 1915– .

Checklists

Checklist bibliographies are designed to list the works dealing with a certain subject or person, such as the following:

Gwinup, Thomas. *Greek and Roman Authors: A Checklist of Criticism,* 2nd ed. 1982.

Weixlmann, Joe. *American Short Fiction Criticism and Scholarship, 1959–1977:* A Checklist, 1982.

Kuntz, Joseph. *Poetry Explication: A Checklist of Interpretation Since 1975 of British and American Poems Past and Present,* 1980.

Salem, James M. *A Guide to Critical Reviews.* I. American drama, 1909–69. II. The Musical, 1909–74. III. Foreign Drama, 1909–77.

Annotated Bibliographies

Annotated bibliographies provide description of the publications to authenticate their editions and identify them, as in the case of the anonymously published books of a forgotten author:

William F. E. Morley. *A Bibliographical Study of Major John Richardson* (Toronto: 1973).

They also help you evaluate the usefulness of a publication for your research:

Drescher, Horst. *The Contemporary English Novel: An Annotated Bibliography of Secondary Sources,* 1973.

Finally, they can provide depth of coverage:

"Shakespeare: An Annotated Bibliography," in *Shakespeare Quarterly* (Autumn 1950). (References are comprehensive with thorough coverage of foreign criticism. Indices to topics, titles of plays, and characters and other proper names.)

Bibliographies of Biographies

Following are examples of bibliographies of biographies:

Slocum, Robert. *Biographical Dictionaries and Related Works, 1967.* (Devoted principally to biographical dictionaries representing all languages and cultures.)
Biography and Genealogy Master Index (consolidated index to more than 3,200,000 biographical sketches in more than 350 current and retrospective biographical dictionaries). *Supplement 1981–82* (more than 1 million additional citations to more than 140 biographical dictionaries).

Bibliographies of Monographic Series

You recall that you can discover the titles of monographic series by author, title, and subject of publications in English through the *Cumulative Book Index*. There is, however, a comprehensive bibliography devoted to monographic series: *Monographic series,* v.1– , 1976– . This is a compilation of Library of Congress printed card catalogs representing all monographs cataloged by the Library. By identifying the individual monographs issued in a series, this catalog serves both as a reference tool and as an acquisitions aid. Popular as well as scholarly series issued anywhere in the world are represented.

For the Periodical

Periodical indices are guides to articles in magazines and newspapers. To determine which periodical indexing service indexes the periodical in which you are interested, look in *Ulrich's International Directory to Periodicals,* which gives the indexing source (if there is one) following the description of publisher, frequency, and price of the periodical.

Periodical indices cover specific subject fields, which are evident by their titles.

Following are listings, under the appropriate divisions, of some of the periodical indices you can find on the reference shelves.

General Research Division (Rms 315 and 108)
Poole's Index to Periodical Literature, 1802–1907
Nineteenth Century Reader's Guide, 1900–1922
Reader's Guide to Periodical Literature, 1905–
International Index to Periodicals, 1907–1965:
    Social Sciences and Humanities Index, 1965–1974
    Humanities Index, 1974–
    Social Sciences Index, 1974–
Bibliographie der deutschen Zeitschriftenliteratur, 1896–1964
Bibliographie der fremdsprachigen Zeitschriftenliteratur Repertoire bibliographique international des revues/International Index to Periodicals, 1911–1964
International Bibliographie der Zeitschriftenliteratur aus allen Gebieten des Wissens, 1963/4–
Education Index, 1929–
Index to Legal Periodicals, 1908–
Index to Foreign Legal Periodicals, 1960–
Index to Religious Periodical Literature, 1949–52
Biography Index, 1947–

Economic and Public Affairs Division (Rm 228)
Business Periodicals Index, 1958–
    (formerly the *Industrial Arts Index,* 1913–57).
Public Affairs Information Service, *Bulletin,* 1915–

Funk and Scott Index to Corporations, 1960–
  F & S Index, Europe, 1978–
  F & S Index, International, 1968–
  F & S Index of Corporate Change, 1978–
Combined Retrospective Index to Journals in Political Science, 1886–
  1974.
United States Political Science Documents, 1975–

Science and Technology Research Center (Rm 121)
Applied Science and Technology Index, 1958–
Agricultural Index, 1919–1964
Biological and Agricultural Index, 1964–
Index Medicus, 1960–

U.S. History, Local History & Genealogy Division (Rm 315N)
Genealogical periodical index, 1962–
American Genealogical-Biographical Index, 1952–

Art and Architecture Collection (Rm 313)
Art Index, 1927–

Slavonic Division (Rm 217)
American Bibliography of Slavic and East European Studies
Letopis zhurnal'nykh statei iretaenzii

Oriental Division (Rm 219)
Guide to Periodical Literature (India)
Fihrist (Arabic)
Turkiye makalslev bibliografyasi (Turkey)
Zasshi Kiji sakuin (Japan)

Music Division, Performing Arts Research Center, NYPL at Lincoln Center (PARC)
Music Index, 1949–

Billy Rose Theatre Collection, PARC
Guide to the Performing Arts, 1957–
Guide to the Musical Arts, 1953–56
Dance Collection, PARC
Guide to Dance Periodicals, 1931/35–1961/62

Schomburg Center
Index to Periodicals by and about Negroes, 1960–

Indices to Newspapers
Index to the *Times* (London)
Index to the *New York Times*
Index to the *Wall St. Journal*
Al-Ahram Index (Cairo)
Letopis gazetnykh statei (for Russia. There are also separate indices for each Soviet republic).
Newspapers are sometimes indexed in periodical indices, i.e., *Funk and Scott Index* includes the *Wall St. Journal* and the *New York Times.* The *Federal Index* includes the *Washington Post.*
Newspapers are indexed in data banks: the *Globe and Mail* (Toronto) and the *New York Times* have individual data bases.
See: Milner, Anita Cheek. *Newspaper Indexes: A Location and Subject Guide for Researchers* (1977).

Indices to Literature Reviews
Some indices are used primarily for reviewing current literature.

General Research Division
Book Review Digest, 1905–   gives brief quotations from reviews of published books and citations to other reviews.
Periodicals such as *Publishers' Weekly, Choice, Library Journal,* and the *Reprint Bulletin* review recent publications.

Economic and Public Affairs Division
Journal of Economic Literature, issued monthly by the American Economic Association, carries book reviews and abstracts of articles and books.
Index to Economic Articles indexes articles and books by subject classification number.

Sciences and Technology Research Center
New Technical Books, 1915–

Indices that Give Abstracts
Abstracts of articles, books, and research papers may be a few lines or a long paragraph. With the ab-

stract you will find the title, date, volume, and page numbers of the publication where the full article or report can be found.

General Research Division

Historical Abstracts: Bibliography of the World's Historical Literature, issued quarterly beginning in 1955, with an annual index covering more than 30 languages and 85 countries, excluding the United States and Canada. Part A: Modern History Abstracts, 1450–1914. Part B: Twentieth Century Abstracts, 1914–

For the United States and Canada use *America: History and Life,* 1964–   . Part A: Article Abstracts and Citations; Part B: Index to Book Reviews; Part C: American History Bibliography (of articles cited in Part A, new books cited in Part B, and dissertations); Annual; Part D: Annual Index (cumulative subject indices to Parts A, B, C, book review index, book title index, list of abstracters, and list of periodicals).

Psychological Abstracts, 1927–

Resources in Education, a monthly abstract "permitting the early identification and acquisition of reports."

Dissertations Abstracts International abstracts MA theses and PhD dissertations from universities around the world and provides a number by which you can order the work in xerox or microform from a central clearinghouse. This appears monthly in two series: humanities and social science series and science series. It relates the latest university research. NYPL no longer acquires dissertations.

Economic and Public Affairs Division

Sociological Abstracts, 1952–

Work Related Abstracts, 1973–

   Employment Relations Abstracts, 1959–72

   Labor Personnel Index, 1950–58

American Statistics Abstracts, 1973–   . You must use its companion volume *The American Statistics Index* to find the abstracts in the *Abstracts* volume. (The Congressional Information Service's *Abstracts to U.S. Government Publications* is a similar publication. See the section on Government Publications.)

Indices to Special Issues of Periodicals

Another form of index that is used as a guide more to current than to past literature is an index that indicates which issues of which periodicals contain special information, such as listings of trade shows, buyers, or dealers; an example is the *Guide to Special Issues and Indexes of Periodicals*. Although issued only every few years, it is valuable for current material because it indicates, for example, that the May 15 issue of *Fortune* magazine lists the top 500 corporations, so that you can seek that issue for the current year to find the latest listing.

Consumers Index (to product evaluations and information sources) provides monthly brief annotations about the articles cited.

For Bibliographical Lists, Citation Indices, Reports

An example of this rarer type of index is *Exchange Bibliographies*, issued by the Committee of Industrial Relations Librarians. It is valuable for the variety and individuality of its approach to subject themes.

Citation Indices
If you wish to find articles that have referred to a certain author and his or her article, the following periodical citation indexes can be used:

Arts and Humanities Citation Index, 1976–
Social Sciences Citation Index, 1972–
Sciences Citation Index, 1961–

Guides to Reports, Research Papers, Conference Proceedings, etc.
Institutions often issue indices to their publications, such as the Conference Board's *Cumulative Index* (in Economic and Public Affairs) and the Rand Institute's *Index* to its reports (in Science and Technology).

The annual *Economic Working Papers Bibliography* lists research papers issued by university research centers and institutes. Research libraries acquire these working papers not in book form, but in microfiche; the *Bibliography* provides the numbers by which they are filed (in Economic and Public Affairs).

Some of the indices for conference proceedings found in the General Research Division are as follows:

Index to Social Sciences and Humanities Proceedings, issued quarterly with annual cumulations with author, editor, corporate, and permutation indices to its main section listing the contents of the published proceedings.

Directory of Published Proceedings guides you to preprints and published proceedings of congresses, conferences, symposia, meetings, seminars, and summer schools held worldwide from 1964 to date, with a location index and subject/sponsor index. These proceedings will be found under the name of the sponsoring organization in the library catalog. For the most part they are cataloged as individual monographs. Sometimes, however, they are treated as a series, in which case you must locate the entry for the first conference in the library catalog and indicate on your request slip the number or date of the conference you want.

World Meetings: Social and Behavioral Sciences, Human Services and Management: a two-year registry of future meetings (quarterly). For future medical, scientific, and technical meetings use

> *World Meetings: United States and Canada*
> *World Meetings: Outside the United States and Canada*
> *World Meetings: Medicine*

For Primary Information and Current Facts

Where most of the foregoing bibliographies and indices include citations to sources you must find somewhere in the library, and hence are indices to secondary sources, there are indices that lead you directly to the information in the same volume or the same series of volumes. *Facts on File, Keesing's Contemporary Archives,* and the *African Economic and Political Research Index* provide quick reference to news events because the information is given in the same volume as the index.

In the same way the many annual almanacs such as the *Information Please Almanac, World Almanac,* and *Whittaker's* (for Great Britain) are indices to facts and addresses. The *World of Learning* lists all institutions (e.g., museums, art galleries, universities, etc.) by country. The *Statesman's Yearbook* includes an index at the back of the volume to the geographic, demographic, social, and economic facts about nations in the remainder of the volume. The *Europa Yearbook* provides the same sort of annual guide to primary information about the world's nations, their institutions, leaders, and statistics.

Many governments issue statistical yearbooks in this category, such as *Statistical Yearbook of the United States, Japan Statistical Yearbook, United Nations Statistical Yearbook, New York State Statistical Yearbook.*

Of course, encyclopedias like the *Britannica* are primary source indices, as are the many biographical dictionaries: *Grove's Dictionary to Musicians*, the *Dictionary of National Biography*, *Current Biography* (in which there is an index to the biographical articles in earlier volumes), and the *Marquis Who's Who Publications Index* listing alphabetically the names of biographies and page numbers to their biographical information in 14 current *Marquis Who's Who* biographical directories.

A final example of a primary-source index is *Art Prices Current*, a record of sales prices at the principal London, Continental, and American auction rooms, 1908–   . (It also indexes artists, engravers, and collectors.)

Current Material

Because periodical indices appear several weeks after the issues of the periodicals they index, for very recent articles you have to look over the list of contents of the current issues of periodicals, which you can get at the library's current periodical desk. To find which periodicals are in your field, use Ulrich's *International Periodicals Directory, Standard Periodicals Directory* (for U.S.A.), *Gale Directory of Publications* (for newspapers), *Black List: Guide to Publications in the Black World, National Directory of Newsletters and Reporting Services, Directory of Business and Financial Services, Bacon's Publicity Checker*.

Some reference works provide information on current activities, such as the *Publishers' Trade List Annual* listing books currently published, by publisher, which is used by authors hoping to sell manuscripts. The *Literary Market Place* gives authors the names of editors to whom to send manuscripts.

Financial investors depend on Standard and Poor's *Corporation Records* for current data on businesses and S&P's *Stock Guides* and *Bond Guides* for current prices. The *Value Line* analyzes firms on the stock markets on a current basis.

There are periodicals devoted to bringing you current articles in translation, such as *Eastern European Economics*, which translates into English. For papers translated into English on various subjects, look for U.S. Joint Publications Research Service (JPRS) *Monographs*, currently announced in *U.S. Government Research and Development Reports* (semimonthly) and listed in the *Monthly Catalog of U.S. Government Publications*.

Libraries maintain current vertical files of clippings from newspapers and magazines, and pamphlets organized under subject headings.

For Special Materials

Microform

U.S. Library of Congress, *National Register of Microform Masters;* a catalog of master microforms that have been produced for the sole purpose of preserving printed material on film (for making other copies), it reports master microforms on foreign and domestic books, pamphlets, serials, foreign doctoral dissertations, but excludes technical reports, typescript translations, foreign or domestic archival manuscript collectibles, U.S. doctoral dissertations, and master's theses.

Guide to Microforms in Print—Subject: Incorporating International Microforms in Print (Westport, Conn.: Microform Review, 1980).

U.S. Library of Congress. *Newspapers in Microform: Foreign Countries, 1948–1972* (The dates given refer to dates of reporting not to dates of original publications. A geographical arrangement of more than 8000 newspaper titles, from all periods, as reported by 258 U.S. and 266 foreign libraries, as well as many commercial firms. All reported locations are given.)

U.S. Library of Congress. *Newspapers in Microform: United States, 1948–1972* (The dates again refer to when the libraries reported holdings to the Library of Congress.)

New York State Library, *Checklist of Newspapers in Microform in the New York State Library* (1979)

A Union List of Selected Microform in Libraries in the New York Metropolitan Area (1979)

Manuscripts

Two forms of guides to manuscript collections exist: (1) those that list the actual manuscripts and their locations; (2) those that list archives and give some idea of the range of subjects of manuscripts found there.

Manuscript Lists:

U.S. Library of Congress, *National Union Catalog of Manuscript Collections,* issued periodically from 1959, gives the location and number of items, and also reports archival materials and manuscript collections in microform.

Hamer's Guide to Archives and Manuscripts in the United States
U.S. National Archives, *Guide*
Great Britain, Public Record Office, *Guide*
For full summaries of records transmitted to the Public Record Office,
see *Reports of the Deputy Keeper of the Records.*
Great Britain. Historical Manuscripts Commission. *Reports* are indexed in its *A Guide to the Reports on Collections of Manuscripts
of private families, corporations and institutions in Great Britain
and Ireland:* Pt. I, "topographical" (cd. 7594), 1914; Pt. II, "Index of Persons, 1870–1911," 1935, 1938; "Index of Persons, 1911–
1957," 1966.
Great Britain. Historical Manuscripts Commission. *Bulletin of the National Register of Archives,* no. 1–   , 1947–

(Since 1923 the Institute of Historical Research, London University,
published in its *Bulletin* lists of migrations of historical manuscripts in
two parts: Part I: Information from booksellers and auctioneers' catalogs about manuscripts, offered for sale; Part II: annual reports from
national and local repositories on manuscripts received by them. Pres-
sure on the *Bulletin* necessitated that Part II be taken over by the Historical Manuscript Commission's *Bulletin of the National Register of
Archives* in 1955. There is an *Index to Lists of Accessions to Repositories,* 1954–58. From 1959, *Lists of Accessions* has been printed as
a separate publication of the Commission. Summaries of all reports
received were printed in the Commission's *Annual Reports.* The Historical Manuscripts Research Centre, Quality Lane, London, provides
an immensely valuable service in locating manuscripts for researchers.
Also the Business Archives Council in London coordinates the collection of papers of firms, banks, institutions, and so on with sister coun-
cils in other European countries and provides a fine reference service.)
  In other European countries institutions individually print catalogs
of their manuscript holdings, which you may find in the library's catalogs either by subject heading or by the institution as corporate-author
main entry. (The Library keeps a separate card file of some of these
publications behind the information desk in the General Research Division.) These countries do not have a national coordinating body that
lists manuscript accessions. The individual publications, however, are
listed in the national bibliographies, which you must search through to
be sure of finding them.

Manuscript Archive Lists:

Location Register (of twentieth-century English language manuscripts and letters), 2 vols. London: British Library, 1988.

Bond's *Guide to the Records of the British Houses of Parliament.* (London: HMSO, 1971).

Grimstead, P.K. *Archives and Manuscript Repositories in the USSR: Moscow and Leningrad,* serves "as a starting point for the foreigner planning research in the Soviet Union," 1972.

Numerous guides like these are found in the catalogs of large research libraries.

Films

U.S. Library of Congress, *Author Catalog,* a cumulative list of works represented by Library of Congress printed cards, 1948–52: for motion pictures and film strips.

1953–57, L.C. National Union Catalog, v. 28
1958–62 the same, vols. 53 and 54
1963–67, 2 separate vols. in the N.U.C. set
1968–72, 4 separate volumes in the N.U.C. set
1973–77, 7 vols. in the N.U.C. set

Films and Other Materials for Projection, 1978–
Audiovisual Materials, 1980–

Photographic and Print Collections

As part of the Library's Wallach Division of Art, Prints, and Photographs Division, the Photographic Collection maintains a card catalog near the Print Collection card catalog in Room 308.

Actual photographs kept in Collections are distinguished from photographs in books. There are several thousand collections of actual photographs in NYPL from the many divisions that have been brought together in a single location. (A collection can have from one to thousands of images. For instance, the Robert Dennis Stereograph [double image] Collection in the New York Public Library has 70,000 images and is international in scope.) The collections have been cataloged separately by photographer, type of issue (format, portfolio, etc.), and added entries (which can amount to as many as 20 subject entries). They are found in a unique catalog.

Photographs in books, however, are found in the general library catalog under the author and the subject of the book. The parts of the collection acquired before 1952 and after 1982 may be located in the collection's shelf list catalog by the call number "MF." The collection acquired between 1952 and 1982, however, was assigned fixed location call numbers, which means they are not together in the shelf list and are therefore not as easy to locate.

Records and Tapes

The Rodgers and Hammerstein Archives of Recorded Sound in the Performing Arts Research Center at Lincoln Center represents a half-million records, tapes, and other forms, 80 percent of which are uncataloged. The items are filed by the name of the Record Company and the number it gave them. They are located through Record Company catalogs and national record catalogs, for instance, *Schwann record and tape guide* (1949–71); *Schwann-1, records and tapes* (1972–Nov. 1983); *Schwann-2* (semiannual supp.); *The new Schwann* (Dec. 1983–   ). In a cooperative venture with the Recorded Sound Index Company, the Archives have been entering accessions onto the RLIN online in recent years. Audio-visual and audio cassette titles are listed with their publishers in *On Cassette* (New York, Bowker, 1986).

For Government Publications

Government publications offer a wealth of information on just about every conceivable subject and are indispensable to economic planners and research consultants to governments and private industry. Researchers in the social sciences also find them indispensable. The problem is how to locate them.

First, you should know that many public research libraries put government publications with the rest of the collection, but they keep guides to these publications and to government archives in special areas. In the NYPL Research Libraries, for example, these guides are shelved in the Economic and Public Affairs Division. Most university libraries, on the other hand, have separate departments for government publications.

Second, governments designate certain libraries as depositories for their "depository" publications, which are free of charge to those libraries. The U.S. government identifies depository publications in the following way:

Depository libraries are permitted to receive one copy of all publications of the U.S. government except those determined by their issuing components to be required for official use only or those required for strictly administrative or operational purposes which have no public interest or educational value, and publications classified for reasons of national security. In addition to the exceptions noted, the so-called cooperative publications, which must necessarily be sold in order to be self-sustaining, are also excluded.

Depository libraries are designated by U.S. Code Title 44 Chap. 19. They include two libraries for each congressional district, two libraries to be designated by each senator in every state, the libraries of land-grant colleges, libraries of independent agencies of government, and libraries of executive departments.

Actually, most depository libraries *select* from among U.S. publications marked for deposit. In New York State, for example, only the State Library in Albany accepts all U.S. government depository publications. As for the U.S. nondepository government publications, because they must be purchased, few libraries have them. Fortunately, research libraries subscribe to the Readex Microprint Service, which provides the full texts of all depository and nondepository publications appearing in the *Monthly Catalog of U.S. Publications* (from 1955 and 1953, respectively) on microprint cards kept in the libraries. By indicating the date of the catalog, the serial number of an item, and whether the item is depository or nondepository, you can get direct access to it.*

As an example of policies of research libraries on government depository material, The New York Public Library's policy is as follows: United States (select depository); Canada (depository for serials and statistics publications); Australia, Netherlands, Sweden (automatic receipt of publications from statistical agencies); United Nations (depository for items from New York); UNESCO (depository for publications from Paris); International Labor Organization (comprehensive subscription); Organization for Economic Cooperation and Development (depository); Organization of American States (comprehensive subscription); state governments: California, New Jersey, New York, Washington (depository); New York City (depository).

*In the *Monthly Catalog* a black dot (i.e., " • item") after the bibliographic description indicates a depository item; no black dot indicates a nondepository item. Look up a depository item in the library catalog, first, to see if the library has it in paper.

Third, you should approach government monographs by the *year of publication;* you can approach government serials as you do other serials, by title or corporate entry.*

Fourth, think of government publications in *geographic terms.* Approach them by country of publication. Within that country, approach them by governmental level—national, state, county, or municipal government. Take the United States as an example: you are confronted with three main indices corresponding to three levels of government.

1. On the federal level: the *Monthly Catalog of United States Government Publications* (Washington, D.C.: Government Printing Office).
2. On the state level: the *Monthly Checklist of State Publications* (Washington, D.C.: Library of Congress).
3. On the local level: the *Index to Current Urban Documents* (Westport, Conn.: Greenwood Press).

At the local level of government (county and municipal publications), the *Index to Current Urban Documents* is issued quarterly, cumulated annually, and arranged geographically with a subject index. If the publications are not held by the research library, you may obtain them on microfiche from the publisher of the *Index.*

You step up to the state government level with the *Monthly Checklist of State Publications,* cumulated with a subject index annually since 1910. This is a selective checklist; for a complete checklist you must consult the guides published by each state. For example, New York State issues the *Checklist of Official Publications of the State of New York* (1947–   ).

For the historical researcher in state publications *(Index of Economic Material in Documents of the States)*** Adelaide Hasse indexed the documents of some states by issuing agency and subject, and listed the titles of legislative documents with their numbers.

On the national level, the profusion of government publications is so great you confront numerous guides to them. We will take these guides in order of relevance to the average researcher:

*The volumes of the NYPL's *Catalog of Government Publications in The Research Libraries* exemplify these approaches by the manner in which the entries are organized.
**This indexes material from the following states, from the establishing of their statehood to 1904: California, Delaware, Illinois, Massachusetts, Kentucky, Maine, New Hampshire, New Jersey, New York, Ohio, Pennsylvania, Rhode Island, Vermont.

1. *Monthly Catalog of U.S. Government Publications.* This is the most complete guide to the publications issued since 1885, although at one time it was said to have missed 40 percent of what was being published. The bibliographic citations to publications appear in the *Monthly Catalog,* about four months after the items are published. Therefore, if a publication was printed late in 1980, you would expect to find it listed in the catalog for 1981.

   The monthly issues have subject, title, and author indices which are cumulated annually. Bibliographical citations to government serials in the *Monthly Catalog* are printed in a separate annual volume. Before June 1976 they were listed in the February issue of each year.

   You should know of the *Cumulative Index,* by subject to the *Monthly Catalogs* from 1900 to 1971—a blessed time-saver for historical researchers.

2. United States, Superintendent of Documents, *Documents Catalogs,* was published annually from 1893 to 1940 and arranged by issuing agency and subject. These volumes give better coverage than the *Monthly Catalogs* for those years.

3. *Ames Index, 1881–1893* provides a subject guide to U.S. government publications for this period.

4. Poore's *A Descriptive Catalog of the Government Publications of the United States, 1774–1881,* is commonly known as "Poore's." Ben Perley Poore described as many publications as he could find, arranged them chronologically by year of issue, and provided a subject index.

   In these guides, you can find congressional committees for hearings, committee reports, and committee prints. You then find the hearings and committee prints by committee in the library catalogs. Congressional reports, however, require an intermediary step: after you have found their report numbers in one of the guides, you must consult the *Numerical Lists* for their volume number in the congressional serial set.

5. *Numerical Lists* are arranged by Congress and Session and then by Senate Documents, House Documents, Senate Reports, and House Reports. Opposite each entry is the volume number of the congressional serial set. Congressional Committee reports are bound in the serial set, the volumes of which are numbered consecutively beginning with the Fifteenth Congress. Reports for the first

14 Congresses are bound in numbered volumes called the *American State Papers*. To request Senate Report 347 of the 72nd Congress, 1st session, for example, you would write down the serial set volume number, that is, 9487 (which you find in the *Numerical List*), and the call number for the serial set (which you find in the library catalog). You will find Senate Report 347 bound in numerical order with other Senate Reports. The Congressional Information Service has published the *U.S. Serial Set Index* (a duplication of the *Numerical Lists* with subject indices) to facilitate research.

6. *Indexes to Congressional Hearings* were issued in volumes, each spanning several years, with the first covering hearings before 1935. They are arranged by Committee and then by subject. If you need the subcommittee name as well, however, use the *Monthly Catalog*.

In the New York Public Library you may have difficulty locating the call number for U.S. congressional hearings. This is because catalog format was changed and hearings have been published on microfiche since the late 1970s.

For congressional hearings held before 1965, look in the NYPL *Catalog of Government Publications in The Research Libraries* (brown volumes) under United States, the name of the main committee (which will be in inverted form for purposes of filing alphabetically) and the Congress and Session [for example: United States. Judiciary Committee (Senate 42:2)].

There was a large backlog of government publications waiting to be cataloged in the 1960s, hence many hearings from that period were cataloged with hearings from the 1970s in the NYPL Research Libraries' *Dictionary Catalog* 1972–1980 (blue) and the *Supplement* 1972–1980 (red). Be careful when you search because these 1972–1980 catalogs are filed alphabetically word by word, including *of* and *the,* so that, for instance, Committee of Labor Affairs, appears before Committee on the Judiciary. Also, you must know the subcommittee to find hearings in the blue and red catalogs, whereas you do not need it for the earlier brown catalog.

From 1978 through 1980, NYPL purchased hearings on microfiche from the Congressional Information Service (CIS) and discarded the paper copies. Therefore, you must locate hearings

Serial
entry
number

Superintendent│of Documents
classification number

FEBRUARY 1963

Judiciary Committee, Senate

2097   Concentration ratios in manufacturing industry, 1958, report prepared by
Bureau of Census for Subcommittee on Antitrust and Monopoly, pt. 2.
iv+453–510 p. (Committee print, 87th Congress, 2d session.) *Paper,
25c.
L.C. card 62–61726   Y 4.J 89/2:M 31/pt.2

Constitutional rights of American Indian, hearings before Subcommittee
on Constitutional Rights, 87th Congress, 1st session pursuant to S. Res.
53. • Item 1042
L.C. card 63–606237   Y 4.J 89/2:In 2/5/pt.1◄─┐
2098   pt.1. Aug. 29–Sept. 1, 1961. 1962. v + 1–284 + xxxi p. il. map.

HBC

UNITED STATES. Judiciary committee (Senate, 87:1)
    Constitutional rights of the American Indian.
Hearings before the Subcommittee on constitutional
rights of the Committee on the judiciary, United
States Senate, Eighty-seventh Congress, first session,
pursuant to S.Res. 53.   Washington, U.S. Govt.
print. off., 1962.   2 v.   fold.map   23 cm.

    Hearing held Aug. 29–Sept. 1, Nov. 25, 29, and–Dec. 2, 1961.
1. Indians, N.A.–Government relations.
NN 3.63f/j OD ED PC,1 SL AH,1 (LC1, X1)

United States.Judiciary committee (Senate, 87:2)
                              SDG
UNITED STATES. Census bureau.
    Concentration ratios in manufacturing industry
1958. Report prepared for the Subcommittee on
antitrust and monopoly of the Committee on the judiciary,
United States Senate. Together with individual
views. Washington, U.S. Govt. print. off., 1962.
2 pts. in 1 v. (xi,510 p.)   24cm.

    "87th Congress, 2d session, Committee print."

1. Industries–Stat.–U.S. I. United States. Judiciary committee
(Senate, 87:2) t. 1962.
NN S 12.65 1/J ODt, I Edt, PC,1. I SL (E)1 (LC1,X1,Z3)

Fig. 3.2   From the *Monthly Catalog of United States Government
Publications* for February 1963 you find that the Senate Judiciary Committee
published hearings on the constitutional rights of American Indians (serial
entry no. 2098).   You then find both first and second parts in the *NYPL
Catalog of Government Publications in the Research Libraries* under
Committee and number of Congress.   The call number is "HBC." Let us
take the entry above it (2097) on concentration ratios as a non–depository
committee print.   You will find it in the *Catalog of Government Publications*
under the entry "United States. Census Bureau."   This is the main entry.
But fortunately it is also cataloged under its added entry, "United States.
Judiciary Committee," by which you locate it.   If the Library had not
acquired this committee print, you could read it on microprint card by citing
"Feb. 1963, 2097, non–depository" as a form of call number.

from the 95th Congress, 2nd Session, and the 96th Congress in the CIS Abstracts volumes, which give you the number for locating the microfiche in the library. Since 1978 the library has not cataloged U.S. congressional hearings.

After 1980 (the 97th Congress and successive Congresses) the U.S. government published congressional hearings on microfiche, and NYPL accepted hearings on microfiche from the government instead of purchasing them from CIS. Therefore, to locate congressional hearings held from 1980 on, you look them up in the *Monthly Catalog* to find their Superintendent of Documents' numbers by which their microfiche is located in the library. These hearings are also not cataloged in the NYPL catalogs.*

7. *Committee prints* are looked up in the *Monthly Catalog.* The catalog gives you the Committee and Subcommittee that issued them, which you use to find them in the library catalogs.

8. *The Congressional Record* contains the debates in Congress, with an index volume to each congressional session. Here you find synopses of bills and can follow their progress through committees into law and find report numbers dealing with these bills. The Commerce Clearing House (CCH) issues a looseleaf service, the *Congressional Index,* which helps you find bills by subject and trace the progress of bills in the current session. Remember that if a bill fails to become law in one Congress it has to be reintroduced at the next Congress to be considered. The CCH *Congressional Index* also gives the voting records of congressmen.

9. *United States Statutes* includes individual laws, issued separately as *slip laws,* such as P.L. 76–82 (Public Law No. 82 of the 76th Congress). These are bound by year, with a subject and popular name index. To reference the laws, however, you should use the *U.S. Code,* which codifies the laws in force under title and section. There are subject and popular name indices to the *U.S. Code.* At the foot of every section of law in the *Code,* there is a reference to the succession of public laws and amendments that led up to the present law (i.e., 75 Stat. 1325, meaning volume 75 of the *United States Statutes,* p. 1325).

*Note, *CIS Index to Unpublished Senate Committee Hearings 18th–88th Congress, 1823–1964* (1986) 5 vols. [More than 7,300 Senate transcripts on microfiche identified by Congress and Committee Code, e.g., (80) SFo–T.76].

10. The *Federal Register* (published daily, with monthly and annual indices) gives the rules and regulations of federal agencies, which are cumulated in the *Code of Federal Regulations* (CFR) under title and part numbers. There is an index to the CFR. Presidential executive orders and proclamations are published in the *Federal Register* and cumulated in separate volumes.

11. *Treaties in Force* consists of a list of treaties and other international agreements of the United States that are in force. It appears annually, arranged by country and then by subject within the country. A paragraph description is given for each treaty, with reference to where the full text can be found [e.g., TIAS (U.S. State Dept. *Treaties and International Agreements Series*); 20 UST 456 (i.e., vol. 20 of the *US Treaties and Other International Agreements* (1950–   ) p. 456); 80 Stat. 200 (i.e., vol. 80 of the U.S. Statutes, p. 200)]. Historically, there is the U.S. State Department's *Subject Index of the Treaty Series and the Executive Agreement Series* (before July 1931).

12. *Government Reports and Announcements Index,* issued periodically, includes PB, AD, PS, and UB reports in the National Technical Information Service (NTIS) series. The *Nuclear Science Abstracts* lists report series from the Department of Energy (DOE), Energy Research Agency (ERA), and the International Nuclear Information System (INIS). The *STAR Index* (Scientific and Technical Aerospace Reports) carries documents of the National Aeronautics and Space Administration (NASA).

13. *Declassified Documents Quarterly Catalog* abstracts and indexes by subject documents made available to the public by U.S. agencies, such as the State Department, the National Security Council, the Central Intelligence Agency, and the White House. The documents on microfiche are found by an identifying number from the *Quarterly Catalog.*

For federal documents kept not in the library, but in government agencies, a useful guide is *Legally Available U.S. Government Information as a Result of the Public Information Act (1970):* vol. 1. Department of Defense and the National Aeronautics and Space Administration, vol. 2. Other U.S. Government Agencies (M. J. Kerbec, ed.; Arlington, Va.; Output Systems, 1970).

Many documents are useful for research, such as court records, business records, and county records; Harry J. Murphy's *Where's*

What; Sources of Information for Federal Investigators (Brookings Institute)* is a guide to these documents.

14. CIS *Index to U.S. Government Publications,* listing by subject and author, provides an identifying number that refers you to its companion volume, the *Abstract.* The *Abstract* provides the name of the issuing office or congressional committee with which the publication can be found in the library catalog. The identifying number also guides you to the microfiche copy. The *Index* and *Abstract* are issued monthly and cumulated annually from 1970.

15. Commerce Clearing House (CCH) *Tax Guide* is a multivolumed, looseleaf service to the federal and state tax laws, organized by year. CCH also publishes the *Tax Cases* series (Prentice-Hall publishes a *Tax Guide* as well).

16. The Bureau of National Affairs (BNA) *Labor Reporter* is a comprehensive guide to labor court cases, arbitration cases, wage and hour cases, unfair labor practice cases, the regulations of federal labor agencies such as the Equal Employment Opportunities Agency, and state labor laws.

For federal court cases generally, see the *Federal Reporter* and the *Federal Supplement.* For state court cases, see the *Reporter* and *Supplement* for each state, for example, the *New York State Reporter.*

British Government Publications

1. *Government Publications Index* lists government publications issued during the year, gives series and monograph numbers (particularly useful for finding the numbers of parliamentary command papers), and provides a subject index.

2. The *Parliamentary Papers* (cataloged as "Great Britain, Parliament, *Sessional papers")* are much used for economic and social studies from 1800 to the present. Special indices cover the nineteenth century. For the twentieth century, use the *Government Publications Index.* Less frequently used, but important, are the House of Lords *Papers,* from 1800, to which there are special subject indices for the nineteenth century.

3. The *Numerical Finding List of British Command Papers Published*

*See also, Craig T. Norback, *The Computer Invasion* (Van Nostrand Reinhold, 1981), to gain access to personal files in federal, state, and local governments.

1833–1961/62, by DiRoma and Rosenthal, lists under parliamentary session command papers by numbers and the corresponding volumes of the *Parliamentary Papers.* Documents librarians update it for their own libraries. After you find the number of the command paper in the *Government Publications Index,* you use the *Finding List* to locate the volume of the *Parliamentary Papers* in which the command paper is found.

4. *Parliamentary Debates* of both houses are in one series with subject indices to each session until 1935, when the Houses began issuing their debates separately.

5. *Parliamentary Journals,* issued from each House beginning in the sixteenth century, are used to trace legislation and reports.

6. For treaties, you can consult *Index to the British and Foreign State Papers,* 1378–1873, 1873–1900, 1900–21, 1922–34, 1935–60, and so on.

7. Great Britain, Public Record Office, *Guide to the Records,* is a broad subject guide to manuscripts from the days of the British Empire.

Other Governments

Other governments issue national bibliographies of their government publications on a monthly or annual basis.

Government gazettes report current decrees and laws.

International governments and organizations appear to use complicated document classification systems. Fortunately, finding the documents is relatively simple.

The United Nations

The UN publishes two distinct sets of publications. (1) sales publications, intended for sale to the general public and, (2) documents—mimeographed publications given agency classification numbers and distributed internally but available for public perusal.

Sales publications are included with their numbers, in annual lists issued by the UN. Because libraries do not catalog UN sales publications, you must use these UN lists to find the sales number of a sales publication to request the item from the library. For example, the *UN Statistical Yearbook* for 1978 is listed chronologically in the UN lists under the statistical yearbook series; its sales number is E/F 79/XVII.1.

The New York Public Library Call number: XFB
ASTOR, LENOX AND TILDEN FOUNDATIONS

Author or
Periodical: United Nations Publications

Book Title: Sales no. E/F 1979. XVII. I

Date/Vol. No.:

Correct and Legible Name and Address Required

	Seat number:
Name Mary Jackson	
Address 31 Main St.	72
City NY NY Zip 10007	
School or Business Allardyce Inc.	form 28s

You look for the call number in the library catalog under "United Nations. Publications. Sales no.—" and copy this entry with the sales and call numbers on the request slip. For instance, in NYPL, "XFB" is the call number for all UN sales number publications (Fig. 3.3). (The Roman Numeral XVII in the sales number differentiates the statistical yearbook series from other series.)

United Nations documents are indexed in the monthly *Index* to the documents of the general assemblies, committees, and special groups of the UN and sister agencies, which is cumulated annually beginning with 1950 (the 1950 volume includes the documents from 1946). Subject and country indices give the document number with which you find the bibliographic entry for the document in the main section of the *Index*. With the year of the *Index* and the document number (i.e., 1977, A/AC.131/SR 290), you can find the document on microcard or microfiche; for recent years the library may have the document on paper. Note that the documents of the UN's affiliate agencies, such as the Food and Agricultural Organization (FAO) and the UN Educational, Scientific and Cultural Organization (UNESCO), are found in this *Index*, but the sales publications of these affiliates are not found in the UN *Sales Publication* series, but are cataloged in the library catalogs like other books and serials.

Other international organizations, such as the Organization for Economic Cooperation and Development (OECD) and the Organization of American States (OAS), issue catalogs identifying their publications; but their approaches differ. For instance, because the OECD tends to publish in paper form you can find its publications through the library catalogs, whereas the OAS tends to issue documents on microfiche, the numbers to which are found in indices.

INTERLIBRARY LOAN

How do you use the interlibrary loan system? Once you are sure your library does not have the publication, check for it in the standard sources mentioned in this section, and note the libraries listed as holding the publication. Next, go to the interlibrary loan division (called Cooperative Services in NYPL) with your information, including the volume and page number in which the publication was listed. If you cannot find a bibliographic reference to the publication in any of the standard bibliographic sources or in the book catalogs of other libraries, the interlibrary loan librarian can search it for you.

Some standard sources are the *National Union Catalog* of pre-1956 imprints, and continuations; The *Union List of Serials,* and continuations (i.e., *New Series Titles);* Winifred Gregory's *American Newspapers, 1821–1936;* Gregory's *List of the Serial Publications of Foreign Governments, 1815–1931; National Register of Microform Masters;* and other titles listed under Microforms on p. 72.

A research library always has arrangements to borrow books not in its collection from another research library, at the request of scholars. With the increase in the cost of purchasing and cataloging books and the availability of telecommunication systems, research libraries now cooperate in the acquisition and lending of books and periodicals in highly organized systems. For instance, The New York Public Library is a member of the Research Libraries Group (RLG), which includes many research libraries in North America that share their library resources through a Research Libraries Information Network (RLIN).

For librarians and scholars, RLIN is a way to search a machine-readable data base that includes not only the equivalent of their library's card catalog, but also the catalogs of other member and user institutions, plus machine readable cataloging produced by the Library of Congress. As with a conventional card catalog, searching can be done by personal name, corporate name, title, and subject heading. But additionally, RLIN users can search by Library of Congress card number, local call number, International Standard Book Number (ISBN), International Standard Serial Number (ISSN), and several special indices for films, maps, sound recordings, musical scores, and serials.

RLIN, therefore, may be used for finding the locations of publications in other libraries from the present back for decades, in addition to the standard sources. If you want an article from a magazine or a section from a book, remember that libraries send up to 50 photocopied pages free of charge to other libraries.

The RLIN terminal is simple to use. The terminal has a television monitor on which information is displayed and a typewriterlike keyboard on which you type instructions. If you wish to request the data base for a book by title, simply type out "fin" for find, then "tp" for title phrase, followed by the title, omitting the first definite article, for example, fin tp keys to the kingdom." To request the book by author, that is, a personal name, you would type "fin pn Cronin, A." If you wish to ask the terminal for author and title, to narrow the search, you would type "fin pn Cronin, A and tp keys to the kingdom."

When you send the message (i.e., depress the SEND or RETURN key), the terminal screen displays the bibliographic citation: Cronin, A. J. The Keys of the Kingdom, and the place, publisher, and date of publication, plus the anagrams of the libraries in RLIN that hold it (a list of anagrams is kept beside the computer). If you see NYPG listed, for example, you know it is in NYPL's collection. You type "par" for partial showing, send the message, and the screen gives you the bibliographic entry in NYPL, including the *call number*. If a number of listings for the book appear on the screen at first, and you see that one of the listings, let us say No. 3, has an NYPG noted with it, you type "par 3."

If a title is long or you are not sure of its wording, you truncate it using the # symbol right after the last letter, which means "include all titles that include among others the words I have typed." If a title has "and" in it, you differentiate it from the command word "and" (e.g., fin pn and tp) by putting quotation marks around the title; for example, to find the title, *Fictive Capital and Fictive Profit,* you type fin tp "fictive capital and fictive profit." If you are not sure whether or not the last word is "profits" or whether there are more words in the title, type: fin tp "fictive capital and fictive profit#."

If you request by corporate author (e.g., Great Britain, Finance Committee) or corporate title (e.g., the U.S. Coast Guard) type "fin cp." for corporate phrase.

If you wish to search by subject heading, type "fin sp," for subject phrase and "sd," for subdivision of the main subject. For example, "fin sp international business and sd New York City" means display on the screen publications dealing with international business in New York City.

If you wish to search a serial, type "res," for resume, to gain access to the serial catalog online. To return to the book catalog, type "res."

Remember to send the message after you type each command.

RLIN can help you find a book about which you have only the vaguest information. For example, we needed a bibliographic citation for an article on the painter Clay Spohn. His mural "The Legend of New Almaden" was reproduced in color on the cover of the book we wanted to find. We remembered only that the book listed murals done by artists in California for the U.S. Work Projects Administration. The librarian of the art division gave RLIN several subject phrases with which to find it, such as "federal art project—California," "U.S. Work Projects Administration—California," but none worked, until he requested "sp federal art project# and tw california" (# is the sign for truncation; tw means title word). The response was "New Deal Art: California" with the publisher and date, "de Saisset Art Gallery and Museum, University of Santa Clara, 1976," and the call number. This proved to be the book we wanted.

Also, RLIN has citations to manuscript collections. To call up the manuscript files, type the following sequence:

cal rlin (cat)	
sel fil amc	(select file American manuscript collection)
fin sp	(i.e., find sp Adams, John)
dis 7	(display item 7 of the Adams mss.)
lon	(long display—this gives tracings)
ful	(full description)
fin fg	(find form genre)

Other Systems

There are three large communications systems that help you locate books for interlibrary loan.

1. OCLC (Online Computer Library Center)

Only seven libraries contract directly with OCLC; the majority of libraries participate through regional library networks. An access computer terminal, it provides shared catalog information for more than 1200 academic libraries and 70 law libraries, giving bibliographic citations and locations for more than 7 million titles. The Library of Congress is a member of OCLC. Several libraries of the City University of New York are hooked up with OCLC. NYPL is not a member, but it has access through METRO (see next section).

2. UTLAS (University of Toronto Library Automation Systems)

Libraries contract directly with UTLAS for services. One consortium of libraries, UNICAT/TELECAT, contracts directly on behalf of its members. NYPL is not a member.

3. WLN [Washington (State) Library Network]

Unlike the others, WLN is not trying to become a national network, but rather is encouraging groups of libraries outside the Pacific Northwest to replicate or transfer the WLN system by purchasing its software and installing it on local computer systems.

OCLC implemented an online Interlibrary Loan Communications subsystem (a message-switching and record-keeping system). The other three utilities have terminal-to-terminal message switching capabilities with which they are developing online interlibrary loan (ILL) modules. Researchers at NYPL can arrange for searches to be made on OCLC through one of the colleges of the City University, who share terminal time with METRO members.

METRO System

The New York Public Library helped develop a cooperative acquisitions and users system with libraries in Greater Metropolitan New York.

If NYPL does not have the publication and you find another library in the New York area does have it (by searching the standard bibliographic sources and RLIN), you ask a librarian for a METRO card, which introduces you to the other library and allows you to consult the publication.

METRO purchases publications and assigns them to member libraries. Many titles are entered in the catalogs of the member libraries, but many are not. You should refer to METRO CAP catalog (of expensive research titles purchases, 1972–79; more than 14,000 individual titles; most of the entries are unduplicated in libraries in the region), or New York Metropolitan Bibliographic Data Base (6 million locations and 860,000 discrete titles).

METRO has an Inter-Share Library Service that makes deliveries between four public library systems (Brooklyn, New York, Queens, Westchester), three school library systems (New York City, Putnam–Northern Westchester, and Yonkers), and METRO libraries located in New York City. METRO also runs a Free Interchange of Photocopies Program.

Sources in Which to Find Publications in Other Libraries

METRO has published useful compendiums:

A *Checklist and Union Catalog of Holdings of Major Published Library Catalogs in METRO Libraries* (351 catalogs of major U.S. libraries)

A *Union List of Selected Microforms in Libraries in the New York Metropolitan Area* (more than 900 entries with the library locations and descriptive notes)

METRO's Directory of Ethnic Library Collections in the New York City Metropolitan Area (23 ethnic groups)

The METRO monthly newsletter, *For Reference,* reports on its new acquisitions, such as the following:

Canterbury, Eng. (Province) *Registers of the Archbishops of Canterbury in Lambeth Palace Library.* 37 vols. in 20 35-mm microfilm reels (administrative transactions and official correspondence from 1279 through 1645)

New York Philharmonic Symphony Society, *Program Notes, 1st–132nd season, 1842–1974* (32 reels of microfilm)

U.S. Committee on Fair Employment Practice, *Selected Documents of*

Records . . . 1941–1946 (1970); 213 reels (useful for research in social and labor history)

It also alerts you to special collections, such as CORECAT: microfiche catalog of the major theological libraries; *Index Iconologicus:* 400 microfiche, compiled by Duke University Art Department, 1980.

METRO issues informative serials, such as Miscellaneous Publication No. 26: "LEX: a Bibliography of Legal Resources for the Layman."

CRL (Center for Research Libraries, Chicago)

NYPL offers another source for interlibrary loan—CRL, an international center for research materials with a collection of more than 3 million volumes, including newspapers, archival materials, and government records in microfilm. CRL has a 17-volume catalog of its holdings, which is available in large research libraries.

CRL can acquire PhD dissertations of foreign universities that are not represented in *Dissertations Abstracts International.* If CRL does not have the dissertation on hand, it can purchase and lend it. The time it takes to acquire a dissertation varies from 6 weeks to several months.

CRL has an arrangement with the British Lending Library, which sends articles from foreign journals in the sciences and social sciences at $5 an article, if you cannot find the journal in North America.

CRL purchases printed materials on microform collected by the co-operating microfilm projects of South Asia, Southeast Asia, Latin America, and Africa. A copy of CRL's microfiche catalog of these projects is kept in NYPL's Microforms Division (Room 315M).

For other CRL services, see the *Handbook of the Center for Research Libraries.*

European Services

In Europe each country has a bibliographic center to which interlibrary loan requests are sent. For instance, the British Libraries Bibliographic Centre in Yorkshire receives requests from libraries in every area of the United Kingdom, searches its bibliographic files for a library that has the desired publication, and forwards the loan request to it.

The national bibliographic centers in Europe arrange for the lending of publications between European countries. In North America the National Library in Ottawa and major research centers in the United States cooperate in interlibrary loan. But there is no lending for private research between continents. You must pay for photocopies of the items, which the foreign library forwards to you through your research center.

Catalog computer search services have sprung up in every European country. For instance, British Libraries Automated Information System (Blaise) contains British books published since 1950, and American and other books cataloged by the Library of Congress since 1968. The Bibliothèque Nationale has a similar search service, Telesystèmes. Many of these systems also carry periodical data bases. For instance, Telesystèmes has FRANCIS, an index to periodical articles, books, and other publications in two sections, one for the humanities, the other for social sciences.

This leads us directly into online searching.

ONLINE COMPUTER SEARCH

Online—a teleprocessing processing system in which data is transmitted immediately from a computer to remote terminals, or vice versa, by means of communications facilities such as common telephone lines. When you are online to the computer, you send a question and receive an answer to that question in a few seconds. This contrasts with batching, in which requests or processing is done in batches, usually overnight. In a batch system you would not receive your answer until the next day.

The Terminal

The terminal has a screen and an attached printer that enables you to produce a record of the search. There are two types of terminals: printing terminals, which are more or less like electric typewriters, and visual display units, which have a cathode ray tube display. Because it is almost a necessity to have a continuous printed record of searches, printing terminals are the more obvious choice.

The online searching process looks like the diagram in Figure 3.4.

Hundreds of terminals can call on the computer at the same time. The magnetic disks store the information. You type your request, and

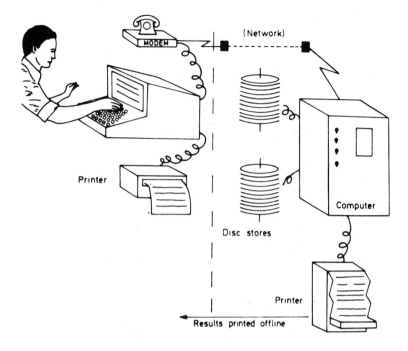

Fig. 3.4

the computer displays the answer. International telecommunications networks carry the message, modems (modulator demodulators) convert the digital messages, which the terminal and the computer understand, to analog messages that can be transmitted over telephone lines. The diagram in Fig. 3.4 illustrates that the display on the terminal may be printed at the terminal or near the computer and mailed to you, as in batch processing.

Networks

Tymnet, Telenet, and Uninet are largely North American telecommunications networks that have hundreds of nodes into which you can dial access to almost all the major American online services. They have nodes in Europe (Brussels, Frankfurt, Geneva, The Hague, London, Paris, Vienna, Rome) and other parts of the world (Hong Kong, Manila, San Juan, Singapore). For example, in Great Britain the Post Office has set up the International Packet Switching Service, which allows British searchers to access computers in North America and North American searchers to access computers in Britain.

(A network node is a minicomputer that does preliminary checks and organizes the sending of messages between searcher and computer.)

Euronet provides access to scientific and technical information for all member countries of the European Community. It links a wide range of existing European information retrieval services, such as the European Space Agency's Information Retrieval, Blaise, Infoline, DIMDI (the West German medical information service), ARIANE (a French service in civil engineering), and ITF (an international textile information service based in Paris); it also links to other networks such as Scannet (operated by Nordfosk, the Scandinavian Council for Applied Research) and can be accessed from North America.

Information Retrieval Services

Information retrieval services are vendors of the information carried over the telecommunications networks. They control online access to this information, which is held in data banks. Among them are DIALOG, owned by the Lockheed Missiles and Space Company, with more than 280 data bases and millions of records; Bibliographic Retrieval Services, Inc. (BRS), which allows full-text searching and access to data bases such as Medlars, ERIC, NTIS; Systems Development Corporation (SDC); and EUSIDIC, which emphasizes data banks originating in Europe.

Data Banks or Data Bases

Data banks, or data bases, are the index sources available in printed book form, which we have discussed as periodical indices and abstracts. New data bases, however, are being developed for access only online. For instance, the printed *PAIS Bulletin* is available in the data bank reached through Dialog information retrieval services; the nonprinted *Executive Information Service* is reached through BRS.

Here are brief descriptions of three data bases, to illustrate what information they provide:

Lexis gives instant access to the opinions in law cases (including the words of the judge in the opinion) and to cases that have been overruled. It includes U.S. Supreme Court cases from 1905, Courts of Appeals cases from 1940, District Courts cases from 1960, National Labor Relations Board cases from 1972, and the Commerce Clearing House *Labor Cases* series.

Nexis gives instant access to the full text of newspapers, magazines, newsletters, and wire services. Newspapers are available the day after they are published, weekly magazines one week after publication, monthly magazines three weeks after publication, and wire services 12 to 48 hours after they are carried over the wire.

Bureau of National Affairs (BNA) provides data bank information on labor contract settlements, basic patterns in the settlements of contracts, work stoppages, National Labor Relations Board election reports, labor arbitration cases, and access, by chemical name, to U.S. government regulations in the Code of Federal Regulations and in the computer tapes of chemical abstracting companies.

All computer retrieval services are somewhat alike, although they differ in that they require their own peculiar computer language. Microcomputers are able to translate computer languages between computer services and thus make available all the data banks in all the information retrieval services around the globe.

You can program your microcomputer for the dial-up procedures, communications protocol, and log-on procedures for the host retrieval systems and specify which system you wish to access. This saves you from having to learn the different procedures for the various systems. Before you connect with the retrieval system you can prepare for your search offline on your microcomputer, to save on the online cost of the search.

You also can store information locally on a microcomputer system, such as scientific abstracts from a large international data base, which saves the cost of repeatedly calling up the data base on the time-sharing telecommunications network.

To make your search, follow these steps (Fig. 3.5):

1. Connect the computer and log on to the online system.
2. Select the file (data base) to be searched.
3. Enter and combine search terms.
4. Print the results.

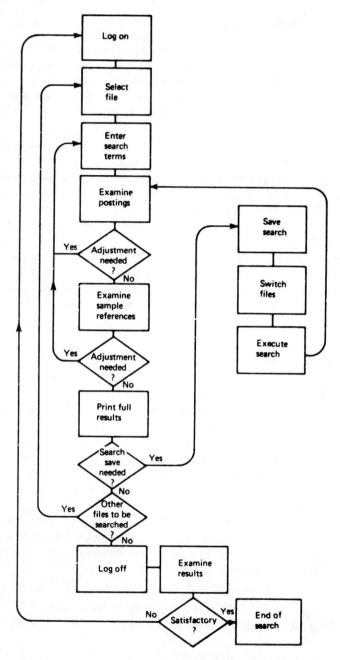

Fig. 3.5

5. Log off and disconnect. (The cost of the search will appear on the
    screen when you log off.)

Specific directions, telephone numbers, and passwords are kept beside
the terminal. You should decide on the descriptors you intend to use
in your request before you connect to the computer, that is, author's
name, title, subjects, or concepts should be clear to you before you
begin.

If, when online, you find that a subject descriptor does not appear
to be finding the number of articles you expected, you may type "e"
for expand, followed by the descriptor. (e.g., "e economic"). A number indicating how frequently it is used as a descriptor appears: "e
economic 5." The computer then displays terms—"economical 25,
economics 510, economist 320"—and you can decide which terms to
use for the best results.

The command language or terminology you use is specific to the
information retrieval service you call on; these can be found in the
manuals you keep beside the terminal.

When you are put through to the system, you are given the date,
the time, and some system news. The system gives you a prompt—
the question mark (?)—to the left of the bottom line, which indicates
the computer is ready to receive information.

You type in the file you want (determined ahead of time by consulting the list of data bases).

Because of the vast amount of information that is instantly available
if you know how to tap it, you must be precise in your questioning;
otherwise, you will be flooded with information you do not want and
be billed for it. You look for key words appropriate to your subject,
and develop connectors with Boolean logic, which is a technique for
performing computer searches by combining or excluding words,
numbers, or characters. For example, AND, OR, and NOT are connectors between subject terms or "concepts," as they are called. AND
means mutually exclusive; CHEESE AND BREAD requests retrieval
of all citations to publications dealing with cheese and bread together,
not to publications dealing with cheese only or bread only. If you want
the latter, you type CHEESE OR BREAD. You introduce NOT into
your command when you want to eliminate a concept: Thus CHEESE
NOT BREAD ensures that you will not get citations to publications
dealing with the making of cheese sandwiches, for example, but you

will get citations to publications on the production and marketing of cheese.

Suppose you approach a retrieval service, such as Dialog. You want to link into DIALOG's data base or data bases that will best answer your question (e.g., What wars have been fought in the Near East in recent years?). You choose the two or three concepts that best represent your question (e.g., Near East and war). You survey the thumbnail descriptions of the data bases to determine the ones you will use, then call up data base DIALINDEX (file 411), which searches all the other data bases in DIALOG. You type the first of the designated file numbers of the data bases you have selected (i.e., File 49, PAIS International) and your concepts, Near East and war. The same is done with each file, in turn [i.e., File 111 (National Newspaper Index), File 132 (Standard and Poor's News)].

The computer tells you how many items of each of your concepts are in each separate data base. From this, you select the data base or data bases with the highest number of "hits" and plug directly into it or them in turn. Type in your concepts "s Near East and war" for "select Near East and war," and carry on the search, expanding or refining it as you go along (Fig. 3.6).

When you have brought your search to the final number of citations, you call up the citations on the screen. You may print them out right away, or if they are many, ask DIALOG to print them and send them to you for less cost.

Strategy

For precision in searching, you need to choose a strategy. First, decide whether to employ the controlled vocabulary, like "Poetry, Romantic—Great Britain," which are unique to each data base, or to use free-text terms, like "romantic (w) poets and English (w) poets" ("w" means with and must be used to link words in the same concept). Controlled vocabulary searches tend to be more formally precise because they pick up items by the subject headings given by the indexers, whereas free-text searches bring a higher recall because, when the whole text of the abstract is searched, the term is more likely to be encountered.

Second, adopt one of three basic strategies: (1) the "building block" strategy, in which you develop concepts separately and then combine

```
*U001   000 CONNECTED TO 41500026


ENTER YOUR DIALOG PASSWORD
xxxxxxxxL LOGON FILE1 FRI 22JUN84
11:48:29 PORTO32


** SORTS ARE NOT WORKING IN 1,10 & 506**
**FILES 139,140,328,648 ARE NOT WORKING*
** FILE 221 IS NOT AVAILABLE ON TYMNET
** OR TELENET                         **
DIALOG NEWS (ENTER ?NEWS FOR DETAILS):
  NEW THIS MONTH:
    ONTAP EMBASE (FILE 272)
  FREE TIME IN JUNE:
    EI ENGINEERING MEETINGS (FILE 165)
      --$49.50 COMBINED CONNECT TIME
    AND TYPES/DISPLAYS
  ANNOUNCEMENTS:
    UNINET AND DIALNET (VIA LONDON)
      MOVED TO DIALOG SYSTEM C
    PRICE CHANGE ON COFFEELINE (FILE
      164) NOW IN EFFECT.
? B 411                                          (Begin file 411, Dialindex)
        22JUN84 11:48:52 USER29432
    $0.20  0.008 HRS FILE1*
    $0.05  UNINET
    $0.25  ESTIMATED TOTAL COST



FILE411:DIALINDEX(TM)
(COPR. DIALOG INF.SER.INC.)                      (I asked for the 3 files at once)
? SF 49 AND SF 111 AND SF 132

UNKNOWN FIELDS:49 AND SF 111 AND SF 132          (But it can handle only one at a
                                                                          time)
NO FILES SELECTED
? S FILES 49                                     (Okay, select File 49, PAIS)

FILE49:PAIS INTERNATIONAL - 76-84/JUN            (Data base is from 1976 through
                                                 the present date in June 1984)
        FILE ITEMS DESCRIPTION
        ---- ----- -----------
? S NEAR EAST AND WAR
      (49)
                758 NEAR EAST
               1749 WAR
               28   NEAR EAST AND WAR            (28 hits)
? S FILES 111

FILE111:NATIONAL NEWSPAPER INDEX -
79-84/JUN

        FILE ITEMS DESCRIPTION
        ---- ----- -----------
? S NEAR EAST AND WAR
      (111)
                4740 NEAR EAST
                8244 WAR
                823  NEAR EAST AND WAR           (823 hits)

? S FILES 132

FILE132:STANDARD & POORS DAILY NEWS, 79-84       (S&P is an unlikely source,
                                                 but check to see if the
        FILE ITEMS DESCRIPTION                   subject is recorded to have
        ---- ----- -----------                   affected the financial market)
? S NEAR EAST AND WAR
      (132)
                0 NEAR EAST
               38 WAR
                0  NEAR EAST AND WAR             (Sure enough: no items)
```

Fig. 3.6 A SAMPLE SEARCH.

```
? S NEAR EAST OR WAR
        (132)
                          0  NEAR EAST
                         38  WAR
                         38     NEAR EAST OR WAR          (A little experimental fun)
? B 111                                                  (Begin file 111)
             22JUN84 11:56:09 USER29432
    $4.3]    0.123 HRS FILE411 6 DESCRIPTORS
    $0.74    UNINET
    $5.05    ESTIMATED TOTAL COST


FILE111:NATIONAL NEWSPAPER INDEX -
79-84/JUN
(COPR. IAC)
          SET  ITEMS  DESCRIPTION
          ---  -----  -----------
? S NEAR EAST AND WAR

                       4740  NEAR EAST
                       8244  WAR
              1         823     NEAR EAST AND WAR         (Type set 1/brief citation (3)/
? T 1/3/1-3                                              first 3 as a sample)
1/3/1
0849769     DATABASE: NNI FILE 111
  AS GULF WAR WORSENS,  TURKEY MAKES BID
TO ACT AS PEACEMAKER BETWEEN IRAN,
IRAQ.  (INTERNATIONAL NEWS)
  DEMIRSAR, METIN; BOWERS, BRENT
  WALL STREET JOURNAL    SECTION 2  P30(W)
P34(E0 MAY 29 1984
  CODEN: WSJOAF
  COL 1    014 COL IN.                                   (The latest entered is the
  ILLUSTRATION; PORTRAIT                                 first out)
  EDITION: TUE


1/3/2
0845150     DATABASE: NNI FILE 111
  SAUDI AIRCRAFT COULD ENTER IRAN-IRAQ
FIGHT.
  OBERDORFER, DON
  WASHINGTON POST    V107  PA1  MAY 20
1984
  COL 1    034 COL IN.
  ILLUSTRATION; PHOTOGRAPH
  EDITION: SUN


1/3/3
0843198     DATABASE: NNI FILE 111
  WAR'S UNCERTAIN EFFECT ON OIL; SUPPLIES
SEEN AS ADEQUATE. (PERSIAN GULF)
  DIAMOND, STUART
  NEW YORK TIMES    V133 P25(N)  PD1(L)
May 30 1984
  CODEN: NYTIA
  COL 3    025 COL IN.
  ILLUSTRATION; MAP; TABLE; GRAPH
  EDITION: WED

? S PY=1979 AND S1                                       (823 items is too many. Limit
              159509  PY=1979                            them to the first year of the
              2       51  PY=1979 AND S1                  data base, 1979) (51 is still
? B 49                                                   too many; I'll come back when
             22JUN84 12:00:24 USER29432                  I think of an additional
    $6.05    0.072 HRS FILE111 3 DISCRIPTORS             descriptor to limit the search.
    $0.43    UNINET                                      Meanwhile, begin file 49)
    $0.30    3 TYPES
    $6.78    ESTIMATED TOTAL COST
```

Fig. 3.6 (CONT.)

```
FILE49:PAIS INTERNATIONAL - 76-84/JUN
(COPR. PAIS INC.)
          SET ITEMS DESCRIPTION
          --- ----- -----------
? S NEAR EAST AND WAR AND S YR=1976
                 758 NEAR EAST
                1749 WAR
                   0 S YR=1976
          1        0 NEAR EAST AND WAR AND
S YR=1976
? S NEAR EAST AND WAR
                 758 NEAR EAST
                1749 WAR
          2       28 NEAR EAST AND WAR
? T 2/3/1-3
2/3/1
   329123   841501124
   THE MIDDLE EAST:
   WAR  DANGERS  AND  RECEDING  PEACE
PROSPECTS  (EMPHASIS ON UNITED STATES
POLICY TOWARD THE REGION).
   FABIAN, LARRY L.
   FOR AFFAIRS ,    62:632-58 NO 3('84),
THIS ISSUE $6.75,
2/3/2
   328220   841306815
   WAR AND "ANTI-PEACE": MIDDLE EAST;
   THE WASHINGTON-TEL AVIV ALLIANCE.
   MEDVEDKO, LEONID.
   NEW TIMES (MOSCOW) ,    P 8-11 NO 2
JA '84,   IL


2/3/3
   308789   831004584
   MORE MUSCLE:  ROLE OF U.S. IN MIDEAST
STRENGTHENS IN WAKE OF THE WAR IN LEBANON;
   ISRAEL'S CRUSHING OF THE PLO (PALESTINE
LIBERATION ORGANIZATION) WEAKENS RADICAL
ARABS AND THEIR SOVIET FRIENDS.

   SEIB, GERALD F.
   WALL ST J ,    200:1+ N 5 '82,

? T 2/5/3
2/5/3
   308789   831004584
   MORE MUSCLE:  ROLE OF U.S. IN MIDEAST
STRENGTHENS IN WAKE OF THE WAR IN LEBANON;
   ISRALEL'S CRUSHING OF THE PLO (PALESTINE
LIBERATION ORGANIZATION) WEAKENS RADICAL
ARABS AND THEIR SOVIET FRIENDS.

   SEIB, GERALD F.
   WALL ST J ,    200:1+ N 5 '82,
   LANGUAGES: ENGL
   DOC TYPE: P
   DESCRIPTORS: *UNITED STATES-- FOREIGN
RELATIONS-- NEAR EAST; *NEAR EAST-- FOREIGN
RELATIONS-- UNITED STATES; *LEBANON--
ISRAELI INVASION, 1982
? LOGOFF
              22JUN84 12:04:18 USER29432
     $4.55  0.066 HRS FILE49 4 DESCRIPTORS
     $0.40  UNINET
     $0.80  4 TYPES
     $5.75  ESTIMATED TOTAL COST

LOGOFF 12:04:19

*U012 000 DISCONNECTED AT REQUEST OF HOST
```

(None of the citations was
in 1976!)

(Only 28 in 7½ years)
(Type set 2/brief citation (3)/
the first 3 items)

I have been using free text
terms. I would like to see what
the controlled vocabulary or
subject headings used by PAIS
would look like; therefore, I
ask the computer to type set
2/full citation (5)/ for the
third item only.

(I am logging-off to plan my
search better. Already the
cost is higher than I expected)

(The host has been DIALOG;
the network has been Uninet)

Fig. 3.6 (CONT.)   101

them with Boolean logic, as we illustrated by the "Near East and war" search example; (2) the "successive fractions" search, in which you begin with a large set on what may be a somewhat vague subject and successively intersect additional concepts to narrow the search to the desired size and specificity; and (3) the "citation pearl growing" search, in which you select a citation known to the data base, examine its index terms, recycle them into the search to retrieve additional citations, and repeat the process until you have formulated a strategy.

VIDEOTEX

Whereas online services provide reference to secondary sources or published literature, videotex presents primary information from a mainframe computer. You select it on the screen from a seemingly unlimited number of frames of information in either text or graphic form. Transmission—by satellite, cable, optical fiber, or telephone links—is displayed on a modified black and white or colored TV set, a multiuse terminal, or a dedicated monitor. Videotex system operators act only as common carriers. Business and nonprofit organizations provide the information.

LEVELS OF RESEARCH

If you want current information or information specific to an institution you probably will use videotex.

If you intend to search a large body of literature for a source that is hard to find or for as many references to a subject you can get, you will use the online retrieval system. It reduces a search that would take days of going through printed sources to a matter of minutes.

If you are searching for a specific topic and, at the same time, remain open to related themes, it is often quicker and much easier to use the printed sources.

WHEN NOT TO USE ONLINE

There are a number of questions you should ask yourself before you use online retrieval:

1. Are there data bases that cover the subject? For example, the best index source for labor relations, trade unions, personnel, fringe

benefits, occupational hazards, and related subjects is the *Work Related Abstracts,* which is not online. There are data bases that cover labor relations, such as the BNA *Labor Reporter,* which concentrates on labor court cases and arbitration awards, and the PAIS *Bulletin,* which emphasizes the public affairs and governmental perspectives. Your question may be answered best by searching the *Work Related Abstracts* volumes in hard copy.

2. Do the data bases provide the kind of information you require? You may be searching for sources for statistics whereas the data bases treating the subject emphasize descriptive and analytic sources.

3. Do they go back far enough? Most data bases emphasize the most current information. Data bases do not go back beyond the period in the late 1970s when the loading of periodical indices onto online began. Some data bases drop sources from earlier years. Therefore, for historical research you have to use hard copy for the most part.

4. Would another source (textbook, abstract journal, encyclopedia, library catalog, telephone call) be better or cheaper? Certainly cheaper, and often faster if the question requires a brief reply.

5. Would an online search be a worthwhile preliminary step even though it could not provide the full answer? You can answer this question only after experience with online searching.

4
Research in Depth

RETRIEVABLE INFORMATION: ANALYZING THE SUBJECT

There are two kinds of researchers. Some work within a deadline and others search until they get the full answer. The first type are responding to the needs or the demands of schools; the searchers after knowledge are usually writing the books and essays of the future or laying the groundwork for other creative works or inventions. The gap between them is enormous. Let us deal first with the harried businesswoman and the frightened college student writing a term paper.

The businesswoman may wish to know whether she should open her retail store to more merchandise. She is interested in the state of her competition, in the changes in her neighborhood, in the general salability of certain products, and in the prospects for small business generally. She knows enough to come to the business section of the library.

In the Economic and Public Affairs Division, she faces row upon row of reference books and tries to remember what questions to ask the librarian. Her time is very limited—not more than two hours every day for one week. She wants current information only, therefore the publications should be quickly accessible. The recent census material is on the open reference shelves. The census of retail trade informs her about her competition; the censuses of population and housing (especially the census tracts) tell her of the social characteristics of her neighborhood; the current industrial reports tell her of the number and value of products manufacturers; the latest volumes of the periodical index, *Predicasts,* forecast growth rates of industries in the economy generally. She turns to the latest *Funk and Scott Index* to find articles about her industry and new products and, because she is pressed for time, she restricts herself to those articles in current issues that can be fetched quickly from the current periodical shelves.

If willing to spend more time, she would select articles from older issues, find their classmarks in the catalog, and while waiting for their delivery look through special bibliographical indices such as the *Cumulative Index* of the Conference Board, an organization that monitors and publishes reports on business and labor conditions.

This reader quickly analyzed her situation into questions that could be dealt with by reference books on the open shelves (found with the help of librarians), and came away within the required time with enough information on which to base a decision.

Another reader with a similar question may begin looking in the library catalog by subject heading, find nothing relevant, turn in frustration to general periodical indices, such as *Readers' Guide,* and search through several years for a few likely references that turn out to be out of date and of no specific help on his subject. "A whole day wasted!" he mutters, and returns to his business none the wiser. He failed to organize his problem into a set of distinct questions, and being unfamiliar with the many sources published by governments, he did not begin his research with the right reference materials. Also, he failed to understand that his time limitations meant he should seek only current materials available on open reference or periodical shelves— and that he should ask for the guidance that librarians are there to give him.

The student term paper writer, on the other hand, usually must do historical research and use the catalogs and periodical indices. But he also is pressed for time. Required to write 25 pages or more on, say, Charles Dickens's place in the development of the novel of social realism, the student must analyze the problem in terms of the availability of information. He must rely on what has already been written. He looks in the library catalog under the subject heading of "DICKENS, CHARLES" to find the bibliographies about his work and the biographies. He looks under the subject "REALISM IN LITERATURE, ENGLISH" for bibliographies and several good books on the subject. If there is any difficulty in locating a specific subject, he should ask a librarian to point out other possible subject headings in that library's catalog. The bibliographies, especially if annotated, help him assess which books are most useful and give references to periodical articles, thus saving the time of poring over years of periodical indices. Also, he looks under the subject heading for social aspects of nineteenth-century England and selects one or two comprehensive treatments. With the books in hand (they have arrived in batches at his seat as he continues to do research in the catalog), he refers to the indices in the back, reads very selectively the pages indicated, and puts down the bibliographic citations of his sources in his notes. If the bibliographies failed to provide him with sufficient references to literary criticism, he may request critical works on English literature of the period, found, again, through subject headings in the library catalog.

Another student required to write about George Eliot's attitude toward women's liberation investigates recent biographies and searches through the past few years of periodical indices, such as the *Humanities Index*. Only as a last resort will he turn to the more general subject headings in the catalog, because the nature of the inquiry is topical and more likely to be found in periodical essays.

Without reflecting on the relation of the problem to the avenues of information in each case, the students might have started in the wrong direction and spent many hours in fruitless research. Poor research can hurt the businessman financially and the student academically, but for the searcher after truth in the long term it can bring disaster.

APPROACHES TO RETRIEVABLE INFORMATION

The Researchers

Are these the men and women of stooped shoulder and weary gait whose lungs are clogged with library air and whose faces and hands are stained with bibliographic rash, the pursuers of dusty books and ancient parchment? No, they are the young and eager, hopeful of finding fame through some area of lore opened to them only through the riches of the library. Or they may be the solace-seekers in refuge for a few hours from the brutal, unmannered world of the twentieth century. They all are our thinkers and, in a sense, our mentors, for what they write shapes our lives. We will analyze their approaches to their subjects in detail.

For the point of view of a famous researcher, read C. Wright Mills's "On Intellectual Craftsmanship" in *Reader in Research Methods for*

Librarianship (1970)—"Seldom does the literature illuminate the sheer joy and intellectual adventure of research."

The Historical Approach

Perhaps the nineteenth century is the period most popular with late twentieth century scholars; in terms of analyzing for retrievable information, it differs tremendously from, say, the sixteenth or the mid-twentieth.

At the beginning of the nineteenth century, the innovations in paper making and printing allowed life to be recorded with a fullness not possible earlier. The records of the time, therefore, are quite extensive, but, because of the infancy and inexperience of most libraries, they are not available now in all research libraries; the researcher faces the problem of locating all the publications to which he has references. On the other hand, the researcher into the sixteenth century is more concerned with locating manuscript collections, particularly letters of the period, and is confined to specific special collections or to manuscript and autograph dealers. The researcher into the midtwentieth century faces the problem of selecting only what is absolutely essential from the mass of printed material available and, at the same time, avoiding any kind of preselection that bibliographic and online services may impose.

Let us, for the sake of illustration, follow a researcher whose subject is a little-known person of the nineteenth century. The man has been a soldier and an inventor, and he wrote for periodicals. He has an Italian name but is English. The researcher had come across a pamphlet of his instructing the English in how to use canes in street fighting. Who was this man? An autobiography is easily located in the catalog but it avoids in-depth treatment, preferring the glamour of adventure. The *Dictionary of National Biography* has no entry for him. The indices to *Notes and Queries* refer to a query about him in the late nineteenth century and a reply from an old gentleman who remembered meeting him at a dinner party 40 years before.

At this point the researcher must think about the time period of his subject. The first half of the nineteenth century buzzed with ideas for inventions discussed in the science and art magazines of the day. The researchers finds by subject heading in the library catalog that the *Me-*

chanics' Magazine is a standard source for that time. He looks through the indices to the *Mechanics' Magazine* of London and finds numerous references to the man and to his ideas for inventions. This man's association with other people is mentioned. A search for the papers of the most prominent of his associates through application to the British Historical Manuscripts Commission brings the researcher to a batch of his letters in the papers of a nobleman preserved in London University. This correspondence leads to other collections of personal papers, all of which reveal the man's politics, deeds, and psychology.

The time was one of great unrest. By checking the guides to manuscript collections of the period's political and labor societies papers, the researcher is able to begin studying the character and politics of the man and his opponents.

The Geographic Approach

Delving into the lives of the man's contemporaries, the researcher discovers that one of the man's daughters married into a prominent family whose name appears as the subject of a family study in the *British Library Catalogue*. The study devotes two pages to the hero's background. With facts from the half-completed autobiographical study of the man's military career, the researcher turns to a geographic approach. He searches for books and articles describing the wars and military campaigns in which the hero took part, and keeps a sharp lookout for footnotes that inform him in which foreign archives papers about the campaigns have been stored. He pores over directories to genealogical archives, and, having corresponded with archivists and located where important materials are held, he researches in those foreign archives for all the papers relevant to the politics, social background, associates, and other aspects of the hero. He may even visit the places where the hero is known to have lived and imagine, with help from local archives, how the scenes must have looked to the hero.

The Subject Approach

The researcher then comes up with a handful of subjects or themes to pursue more deeply. That is, he must now read into the background of the wars, inventions, and themes that he finds significant, to understand their origin and why the hero became involved with them. The result of his research should bring the eventual reader of his book to an understanding of the man and his time that the man himself could never have had.

Other Approaches

The interpretive approach is used when all the facts are available, such as in the archives of a company. The researcher's interpretation of the company's history depends on her general knowledge of the company's competitors, the business climate, and the acumen of the entrepreneurs. If the researcher must discuss a period of the literature, her interpretive approach should be from one of several possible points of view—the symbolic, the biographical, the social-political, the literary-historical, or some other. From here, she can readily discover the availability of retrievable information through bibliographies and the subject entries in library catalogs.

The exclusionary or renunciatory approach requires the researcher to choose, from a great many, one overriding message she wishes to communicate from a plethora of material. The filmmaker of a 90-minute film on the life of Picasso admitted that renunciation was her guideline whereby she ruthlessly excised interesting facets of Picasso's life to give the film shape and meaning. It is an approach adopted by modern-day historians. Unlike Gibbon, they strive not for the whole picture, but merely to contribute to an overall view that later generations may form. Their contributions, however, are satisfying and appear complete to their contemporaries. They therefore research only those aspects that enhance or illuminate the point of view they wish to express.

WHEN TO USE BIBLIOGRAPHIES, INDICES, BOOKS, PERIODICALS, AND MANUSCRIPTS AS EXEMPLIFIED BY SUBJECT AREA

General Knowledge

Sometimes researchers must use all the departments of a research library to track down a subject. The foregoing example of the Englishman who was soldier, inventor, and writer is a case in point. The

military and literary books and articles would be found in the humanities division, whereas a search into his inventions would be done through
periodical indices in the science and the patents divisions.

Another example of a search for general knowledge is the professor
gathering material for a book on the mosquito. Like the mosquito,
information about it and its effect on humans could appear in any
room in the library. The professor spent many hours hunting down
government publications in the Economic and Public Affairs Division
in The New York Public Library, and, in fact, used all the divisions
including Rare Books and Manuscripts. Since NYPL does not hold
medical books, he spent months in the New York Academy of Medicine Library, which is open to the public. For the legal implications
of mosquitos, to be found in legal publications too specialized for
NYPL, he visited the New York University Law Library with a METRO
card. After three years, the professor had written three shopping bags
full of manuscript and was looking for a publisher.

Let us, for the sake of presenting a case closer to the average, follow a free-lance writer who is under a long-term contract to a publisher to produce a definitive book on the continent of Atlantis. The
subject will lead him into mythology, archeology, literature, voyages
of discovery, studies of cultures, economic history, biography, and
fields he could not imagine when he commences his research. He does
not know how he will present the subject, but, from what he supposed
about it, he begins to analyze it in terms of where he can get the
information.

He chooses two areas of reading: the mythology of Atlantis and the
literature of explorers who have looked for it. These two areas seem
to balance one another, as part of the mythology comes from historians of the ancient world and the voyages of discovery are based on
facts gleaned from mythology. They will touch on other areas of research, of course, but these new references the researcher must note
and put aside, regardless of their fascination, until he has exhausted
his research in the first two areas. No doubt, he has already determined that the archeological will be his third approach, but whatever
follows that depends on the revelations of his research.

He begins by consulting the subject headings in the library catalogs
for works on mythology and narrations of discovery. These give him
background, bibliographic references, and scores of ideas. He turns to
periodical literature, starting with the latest indices and working back-

wards. By starting with the latest articles in both fields, he may come across references to earlier articles that were not indexed. The only index to nineteenth century periodicals with any claim to comprehensiveness is *Poole's Index*. Many other periodicals kept their own indices. Haskell's guide *(A Checklist of Cumulative Indexes to Periodicals in the New York Public Library)* is important for its listing of French and German periodical indices; a searcher, to research such a subject, should read a few modern languages.

A good research library should have complete runs of foreign periodicals or be able to borrow microfilm reels of periodicals from other libraries.

The monotony of research may be felt after a time, so that the researcher who began with two fields may be grateful that he can change from mythology to personal adventure and back again. The bulk of personal adventure probably remains unpublished, but if it was at all important, it might be located in manuscript collections throughout Europe and America. The researcher may welcome this respite from his reading as he looks through directories to archives and libraries for various countries, catalogs and guides to special collections, and bibliographies of works and manuscripts on exploration through the centuries.

He writes to the archivists of special collections he wishes to visit. This correspondence may lead him to other collections, the existence of which he could not have known about, and to scholars in the field who, for the most part, will respond to his queries with useful suggestions. By this point, he has only touched the tip of the iceberg.

His visits to manuscript collections bring him a wealth of material, all of which he may spend some weeks assimiliating before he goes on to the archeological approach. As any casual reader of periodical literature knows, there have been several discoveries of "Atlantis" in recent years. The archeological reports of these expeditions are published in the papers of archeological societies; personal reports of the expedition members may be lodged with the organizations that sponsored the expeditions. No doubt the researcher will have noted down many archeological sources from his primary reading. He may wish to find biographical information about expedition leaders to assess their motivations. Major newspapers often provide such information, and local newspapers from an archeologist's birthplace sometimes provide interesting facts found nowhere else. Through the membership lists of professional organizations, the researcher may locate archeologists for correspondence or interviews, though this type of research is best left to last, when the researcher feels he knows everything he needs to know to ask pertinent questions. Visits to the archeological sites, however, may be considered important at any time during the research, because the researcher will find the necessity of keeping his reading (which gives him an abstract view of the subject) in touch with the reality.

A study of the cultures, religions, and philosophies of peoples contemporaneous with the archeological sites may be helpful at this point. Through the subject entries in the library catalogs and standard encyclopedias, the researcher locates basic readings, but he may have to visit special libraries like the New York Union Theological Seminary Library, which is open to the public, to find the most informative material.

By comparing the artifacts from the site with the concepts of surrounding cultures, including the economic and legal aspects, the researcher may be able to interpret the culture in question and assess its discoverers' claims that it is the missing Atlantis. The researcher must constantly interpret the facts, and the validity of claims and counterclaims. Sometimes he must go back over his reading to make a reassessment. His notes, kept either on index cards or in notebooks, if sufficiently explicit, can save him much precious time. Also helpful is a special notebook in which he records his impressions from his research as he goes along.

Always, by the way, *keep complete bibliographic citations on every source*—down to the page number.

There is probably literature that evaluates the various Atlantis sites in terms of mythological or ancient description. The researcher should save the works of these commentators to read at the end of his research so as not to be influenced by it and to be able to argue authoritatively with it. Also, these references may provide insights or further leads that he can now chase down quickly and easily.

Humanities

Research in the humanities is largely interpretive but based on the knowledge of fundamental facts that may require the researcher to delve into several disciplines. A PhD candidate searching for the true significance of the poetry of Alfred Lord Tennyson, the literary Picasso of the nineteenth century, may have to read the works of philosophers with influence in his day, biographies of the Tennyson family, and technical works on the phenomenon of memory so implicit in Tennyson's work. A thorough knowledge of the poetic works of Tennyson's immediate predecessors and contemporaries, in particular of Wordsworth, is a prerequisite to a study of Tennyson's poetry.

The researcher, therefore, would begin by consulting the bibliographies of the works of the poets and selecting the best critical works. She would consult the *Dissertations Abstracts* to see if research similar to what she plans has already been done, or if other dissertations may be of help to her. She works her way through a study of the poems she already appreciates by reading the poetry more carefully, the poet's biography, and the critics' judgments, and searching out the poet's techniques through background reading.

Literary interpretation is a slow process. After reading for a couple of years and attempting to express in writing her insights into the poetry gained from her reading, the researcher feels that she has entered the mind of Tennyson and is awake to his sensibilities. She finds the greatest delight in being able to show how erroneous were the judgments of previous critics; it makes the bond between Tennyson and herself seem stronger.

Although after the initial period of research the researcher does not consult the library catalog as frequently, she regards the library as an essential support that at any time could present her with new literary works and articles relevant to her quest. For this reason she visits the current periodical room for literary magazines and review papers, such as the *Times Literary Supplement*. By this time the librarians in the humanities division may become aware of her field of research and draw her attention to recent publications. The library becomes her "home away from home." For further discussion of the route to productive research in the humanities, see Charles S. Singleton, *Interpretation, Theory and Practice* (1969).

Social Sciences

In the late nineteenth century the social sciences began to overtake the humanities in importance and relevance to the world around us. Research libraries do not reflect this change of status because their role is historical as well as topical, but they have had to devote an increasingly larger amount of shelf space in the stacks to social science publications, since the space provided in the social science departments was swamped long ago.

Social science subjects can be interdisciplinary; for example, the voting habits of the English, as political science, touches on economic history statistics and sociology. They can also be singular, such as econometric forecasting techniques. Social sciences have also laid claim to subject fields traditionally conceived as part of the humanities. Law, for instance, is related in many ways to various social science compartments: housing law is central to the socioeconomic struggle between landlords and tenants; consumer law concerns the people versus the retailers; sociologists deal every day with family court law, civil rights law, criminal law, and so on; international law relates to economists and political scientists; labor law relates to personnel managers, labor organizers, and contract negotiators. The same can be said of history and philosophy: economic and political-social history are supplanting the general history books, and the economic-sociological changes in philosophy, with the influence of Hegel, Feuerbach, and Marx, have virtually revolutionized the subject as a social science.

As a consequence of the feverish and exciting intellectual activity taking place in all these fields, the numerous periodical indices offer woefully inadequate coverage. The online data services merely give faster access to the indices. A large part of social sciences publications, because of either their ephemeralness or their political point of view, are overlooked by librarians and their colleagues the indexers and abstracters. The researcher in the social sciences, therefore, must scrutinize the back pages of periodicals for advertisements or references to publications unknown to him or to the library and locate specialized libraries that are likely to have collected them. For publications of the political left, for example, certain church libraries can provide significant literature found nowhere else.

As an example of social sciences research, let us watch a political economist develop a case study to illustrate his theory about how technological diffusion (the disseminating of an invention) takes place.

The case study is the development of the automobile, which was invented in England in the 1820s by Goldsworthy Gurney but was not successfully diffused until the 1890s. The researcher wants to find the reasons for the delay.

First, he notes what the *Dictionary of National Biography* says about Goldsworthy Gurney and looks up the references given by the article about him. Since Goldsworthy was a Cornishman, he looks in Boase's *Bibliotheca Cornubiensis* and finds a long list of writings by Goldsworthy. In them Goldsworthy refers to parliamentary committees, the reports and evidence of which the researcher finds through the indices to the *Sessional Papers* of the British House of Commons for the nineteenth century.

Finding that the steam automobile was repressed by parliament, the researcher searches through the *Journals* of the Lords and Commons for the bills introduced on its behalf and against it throughout the century. Through the indices to parliamentary debates he discovers who is for the steam carriage and who is against it; he discovers that the *Mirror of Parliament* records the votes on important bills, that *Dod's Parliamentary Companion* gives biographical sketches of parliamentarians, and that the railway manuals list railway directors who are members of Parliament. He returns to the library catalog for books on the early railway and their entrepreneurs, and on English banking, English investment abroad, and Belgian and French banking in railways, which sprang up in the wake of British export of capital and machinery to those countries.

He finds that by alternating his research between the political-economic forces and the men who led them, he has developed a good idea of the class factions that opposed the railway to the automobile, but he needs a better idea of their motivation, which he feels only manuscript material can offer. He searches through the Great Britain Historical Records Commission's lists of manuscript acquisitions, which are annual listings of private papers turned over to county archives. Here he finds papers relevant to his themes and writes to the archives in question to ascertain their size and learn more about their subject matter.

Always write before visiting archives, to forewarn the archivist, to make sure the papers have not been transferred, to be sure they relate to what you want, and to learn the hours and days the archives are open.

While in England, the researcher consults the British Library Catalog, including its special subject-heading book catalogs, which are excellent tools for locating books of the early nineteenth century, surpassed only by the subject-heading book catalog of the Library of the

London School of Economics, which he also consults. The latter library has an excellent collection of German and French economic books of the period that the researcher finds invaluable for background information to his theme.

The mass of information is now immense and the researcher has not touched the periodical literature. After chancing on the papers of the capitalist entrepreneur behind Gurney's automobile in a county archives and the papers of another early automobilist in a library of one of the colleges of London University, he must try to establish the relationship of the particular entrepreneurs to the changing society of the industrial revolution. This he cannot do without an economic theory, which begins to evolve from his findings as he reflects on the meaning of the economic and political factionalism. He reads the economics of technological diffusion, the readings for which he finds from the library catalog's subject heading, and the *Index to Economic Articles*. The more he reads, the more he discovers that only Marxist economics has the analytical tools to explain the suppression of the automobile, but, because Marxist economics has not developed a theory of technological diffusion he must develop one from his research within the Marxist economic framework.

One cannot research a theory; however, one can hope to absorb a theory or philosophy by reading the works of its progenitor and its commentators. In the case of the researcher, this must be done when he is relaxing from the strain of his concentrated research.

He discovers bibliographies given as reference sources in books on automobiles in France, the petroleum engine and its inventor Gottfried Daimler, which lead him to significant material in the Bibliothèque Nationale and the Archives Nationales in Paris.

Through a study of the price wars over petroleum among the Rockefellers, Rothschilds, and Nobels, he discovers why the petroleum automobile was promoted by the end of the century and, through a study of the changing class structure in France, he understands why the automobile was allowed to be diffused widely.

By this time he has developed a sixth sense of where material may be found. From Haskell's Guide to periodical indices he is able to pick out the European magazines and time periods most useful to him. He can tell by the title of a book if it is likely to be sufficiently useful.

While writing his book, he will come upon small lacunae in his research that the library's collection can fill and he will stumble on information in the new issues of periodicals.

Since he is writing about automobiles and railways he will have had to visit the science division to read about their construction and their workings throughout the nineteenth century.

Sciences

Most science collections are set up for the use of the knowledgeable scientists. The New York Public Library's Science and Technology Research Center, however, is prized for making science accessible to the beginning student and carrying him through to the most sophisticated works. The inventor of xerography, for example, taught himself the sciences of mechanics and chemistry there.

Much of scientific research depends on searching the periodical literature such as the *Applied Science and Technology Index*. With the coming of computerization, this search for references has become sophisticated and, consequently, is used by scientists whose knowledge allows them to research at a high level.

A researcher in the textile industry, for instance, is looking for the latest scientific techniques, which he finds only through reading articles by a writer working in the trade or maintaining a close relationship with it. The periodical indices do not index all the periodicals, especially newspapers, which the researchers must go through issue by issue. The *Gale Directory of Publications* gives him the title of trade periodicals, and the *Standard Directory of Periodicals* lists magazines by subject field.

The NYPL Patents Collection records all patents taken out anywhere in the world and is consulted by inventors who depend on a knowledge of the past and of the changing social conditions that may allow new concepts of construction or the discovery of new metals to make viable an invention that has lain in the Patents Books for years.

Research in science, however, can lead to the in-depth study of one or several of its many disciplines that requires research in specialized libraries. A directory to guide the researcher to these libraries is *Directory of Special Libraries and Information Centers* (Gale; 4 v.).

Special Collections

In recent years the holdings of special collections in research and university libraries have been photocopied in book catalogs and distributed widely, thus facilitating research. Directories of special collections classify them by subject, so that the researcher first finds their names and locations and then looks in the research library catalog for a listing of the book catalogs of whatever special collections he wishes to see. In New York City, for example, there is the New-York Historical Society, which has had its card catalog of manuscripts of old New York State, including the colonial days, put into book form.

As for what these special collections comprise, let us, as an example, look at the special collections of The New York Public Library.

The Rare Book Room
The Rare Book Room identifies rare books as monographs or serials published in Europe before 1601, in England before 1641, in the Americas before 1801, or modern fine printing. Being scarce does not usually qualify a publication for this collection if it was published after that date; such books are kept in the general stack area unless they are considered particularly valuable. A significant exception is the collection of modern fine printing—private press books designed by such important figures as Bruce Rogers, and books issued by distinguished book clubs. Researchers in rare books depend much on bibliographies in their subject fields, although there is a rare book card catalog with subject entries. Rare printed books, which are consulted not only for the information they give but for the style of calligraphy or printing, the texture of paper, and the method of binding, which informs the cognoscenti of the society in which it was produced and of the school of printing or period of artistry to which it belongs, are valued for their artifactual as well as their textual interest.

Textual research is fundamental to the training of a scholar. The methodology of textual research is taught at Oxford University, for example, which awards successful students with a B.Litt. degree, a prerequisite for the Oxford Ph.D., regardless of the number of Ph.D.s a student may have attained elsewhere.

Textual criticism has several aims. A researcher who hopes to lecture on the political factionalism among Tibetan religious orders may have to consult the book manuscripts of ancient Tibet on early religious tenets in the Rare Book Room. Other scholars compare the various texts of an author's work, both in manuscript and published forms, to trace his artistic development, or to establish a definitive text when an editor took liberties in preparing the work for publication.

On the subject of discovering influences on artists, Lord Tennyson provides us with a good example of a poet who, when his early poetry was strongly criticized, refused to publish for years and reworked his poems. For instance, the versions of "The Lotus Eaters" published in 1833 and in 1842 differ markedly. The textual critic studies Tennyson's many drafts and editorial corrections in the poems throughout the years and researches the events and emotions of the poet's personal life and the social changes he lived through to understand the changes in the poem.

Variorum texts, on the other hand, carry all the changes in the text made by the author (or editors) and therefore require most students to study only the printed editions.

Years ago the textual critic reprinted her idea of the pure or best version of the poem with one or two variants in brackets, but in recent years, under the influence of American scholarship, poems have been reproduced with all variants in the margins of the same page. This is called the *workshop approach,* meaning that all the word tools that were used to construct the poem may be seen at once to give a comprehensive view of the artist's creative development.

Such a study involves the discipline of linguistics and a profound knowledge of the culture. The researcher should collect all the variants of the work in question and then read the correspondence of the artist. Published biographies and critical works of the artist can lead the researcher to collections of unpublished correspondence, but she must query any likely special manuscript collections as well. In the course of researching an artist's life, the researcher may be led to manuscripts of court trials and probate records in the Public Record Office. She must chase down every clue promising revelation until she is satisfied that she has a thorough knowledge of her subject. Then she searches out the book reviews in the periodicals of the day, and peruses them to give herself a feeling for the times.

Literature

Aside from collecting the printed works and correspondence of authors, special literary collections like the Berg or Pforzheimer Collections at The New York Public Library collect the handwritten and typewritten manuscripts of their books. When I saw the typescript of D. H. Lawrence's novel *Kangaroo* in the Berg Collection, I was surprised by its clean look because I knew that he had written it at top speed in a short time. Recently, however, I read that he always sent his work to be typed by others, and consequently, his handwritten manuscript with the corrections he made before it reached the typist alone would reveal his method of working. Revised typescripts, though, like Virginia Woolf's in the same collection, do tell such a story. The library purchases these manuscripts or receives them as gifts from the authors, their heirs, or collectors. Sometimes, as in the case of the letters and manuscripts of the poet W. H. Auden, a complicated court case is fought over their custody. In Auden's case, the court after the friend's death where the poet's friend was his heir, recognized the Berg Collection as the recipient of the gift of the friend.

Just as in the Rare Book Room we find scholars at work on variorum editions of older texts, we might find scholars at work in the Berg or Pforzheimer Collections on textual criticism. Or find both, on odd days, in Manuscripts and Archives.

Manuscripts
From large collections of material, such as the papers of the American Loyalists on their losses from the Revolutionary War, to single autograph letters (i.e., a note from the nineteenth century poet George Foster, "Yankee Doodle will meet you for lunch."), the Manuscripts and Archives section reaches out for all subjects. It has its own card catalog and its own typewritten guides to particular collections. Manuscripts and Archives is especially useful for diaries, which can provide unique descriptions of a period the researcher hopes to understand. It may house all the papers of a particular personality such as the New York socialist politician of the first half of the twentieth century Norman Thomas.

There are manuscript libraries that specialize in particular subjects. For instance, the Schomburg Center for Research in Black Culture has a good collection of Haitian manuscripts, collections from the Caribbean, and from New York's Harlem. The Library's Billy Rose Theater Collection at Lincoln Center has prompt books, correspondence of theatre people, old newspaper clippings, playbills, and photographs— all of which are useful to a researcher.

Finding the whereabouts of correspondence can be difficult. *Hamer's Guide to Archives and Manuscripts in the United States* and the *National Union Catalog of Manuscript Collections* (Library of Congress), issued periodically from 1959, name the library where the correspondence is kept and the number of items, but these merely touch on the great number of archives. In Britain the Historical Manuscripts Research Centre in Quality Lane provides an immensely valuable service in locating manuscripts for researchers. Indeed, Europeans are working together to collect, preserve, and publish guides to their archives. They have made more progress in preserving business archives (i.e., The Business Archives Council) than North Americans have. The British Museum Library publishes guides to its manuscripts; local history associations publish parish records. There are also guides to diplomatic archives (see Daniel H. Thomas and Lynn M. Case, *Guide to the Diplomatic Archives of Western Europe*, Philadelphia: University of Pennsylvania, 1959).

Many manuscripts are in private hands and may be traced through the catalogs and records of sale by commercial firms, such as Sotheby's and Parke-Bernet, or in the advertisements and brochures published by small antiquarian auctioneers. Rare books may also be found in this manner. Some research libraries preserve these catalogs, which are helpful in identifying various editions of a work and locating purchases of rare materials. Private collectors usually permit scholars to see the rare works in their collections.

Genealogy

A multitude of biographical dictionaries and directories, including the *New York Times* Obituaries volume, are part of genealogical research, although they are not usually found in the genealogical departments. Books and pamphlets on families by genealogists fill the shelves of NYPL's U.S. History, Local History and Genealogy Division, as do city directories, county, and parish records, editions of Burke's *Peerage* and *Landed Gentry,* census records, and many others.

Once ensconced in the division, genealogical researchers rarely research outside it save to travel to distant places to inspect local archives, courthouse records, and other genealogical collections. Occasionally you can avoid traveling. For instance, the mecca for genealogists is the Mormon Archives in Salt Lake City, Utah. Many genealogy divisions, like NYPL's, carry the Mormon's *International Genealogical Index,* the 1984 edition of which has 88 million names on microfiche. You look up a name under a major locality. When you find a reference to a parish register or other kind of record, you go to the Library of the Mormon Temple on 65th St. and Broadway in New York City. Through it you can borrow the record on microfilm from the Archives in Salt Lake City. About 9 million names are added to the index every year. A useful guide is Timothy Beard's *How to Find Your Family Roots* (New York: McGraw-Hill, 1977).

This kind of research most closely approaches detective work, which calls for a basic skepticism. Genealogic research is complex; the few guides just skim the surface. To illustrate its complexities, let us look closely at U.S. Censuses and passenger records.

U.S. Name Censuses. The name censuses taken in the United States every 10 years from 1790 (the first true census anywhere in the world) to 1910 are available on microfilm. (Information on names in later censuses may be obtained by writing to the Personal Census Records Office, Bureau of Census, Pittsburgh, Kansas.) The 1920 census of names will be released in 1990. The 1890 census of names was largely destroyed by a fire at the Department of Commerce in 1921. For the early censuses, only the names of the heads of households are given.

From 1790 to 1850 there are indices by name for each state that direct you to the reel and page number of the national censuses. For the name censuses of 1860 and 1870, you can use city directories to find the residence of the individual, then use maps to determine the Assembly District or political division. The New York maps for 1860 give you the reel and page numbers directly; for New York in 1870 you must use the maps and then a guide that gives you the reel and page number. Other states have compiled similar maps as keys to the censuses found at their Genealogical Society Libraries.

For the 1880 name census for New York several steps must be taken to find the reel and page number: (1) Check the name in the 1880–81 New York City residential directory for the home address. (2) In the same directory, in the attached city register section, check the street directory for the exact location of the address. (3) Locate the address on the enclosed assembly district maps (with the large numbers), noting also the election district (small black numbers). (4) Locate the corresponding assembly and election districts on the enclosed tables. Follow the line across to the enumeration district and finally to the reel number. (5) Fill out the call slip with the classmark, *ZI-50, and the reel number. (6) In the upper lefthand corner of each census schedule is the enumeration district. The schedules are arranged numerically by enumeration districts. Check the district schedule for the address of the person or family you seek. The desired information should be here, providing the subject resided at the given address at the time the census was taken—about June 1, 1880.

The 1900 names census has a Soundex approach, which is a system of coding surnames by number. (Libraries can provide you with the detailed instructions.) From the code you can find the reel and page numbers to the microfilm.

For the 1910 name census, you use the city directories to find the street address, then proceed to a guide indexed by street to find the election district. When you have the election district, the same guide gives you the reel and page numbers on the microfilm.

NYPL's U.S. History, Local History and Genealogy Division has a card index (by geographical area) to published censuses and local name surveys from colonial times to 1910.

Passenger Lists. Passenger Lists are on microfilm in the National Archives in Washington, D.C. If you know the name of the vessel and approximate time of arrival and the port of arrival, you can find the passenger rather easily. Research libraries have many of these microfilms; for instance, NYPL has the *Register of Vessels Arriving at the Port of New York, 1789–1919,* in 27 reels arranged by date.

There are a number of indices to these passenger lists, some specialized by ethnic group and others by time period. The following larger indices are organized by surname:

U.S. National Archives
Index to Passenger Lists of Vessels Arriving at New York, 1820–1846 (Washington, D.C., 1958; 103 reels)
Index to Passenger Lists of Vessels Arriving at New York, June 16, 1897–June 30, 1902 (many reels)
Alphabetical Index to Passengers, 1906–1942 (in book volumes at the National Archives)

Some helpful guides are:

P. William Filby (with Mary K. Meyer), *Passenger and Immigration Lists Index* (a guide to published arrival records of about 500,000 passengers who came to the United States and Canada in the seventeenth, eighteenth, and nineteenth centuries; Detroit: Gale, 1981; annual supplements)
Passenger and Immigration Lists Bibliography, 1538–1900 (a guide

QUINN, John (1869-1924)

P Kavanagh pub on home-made press vol of ex-
cerpts from Quinn's literary lrs by memorizing them
after readings in NY Pub Library; Quinn's will
gave lrs to Library on condition they be read by
scholars but not copied or pub till '88; Kavanagh
comments, Ja 17,1:3; ct, at Library request, orders
Kavanagh to show cause why books should not be
destroyed; Library dir Freehafer comments, Ja 21,
28:6; ed, Ja 22,26:2; lr, Ja 25,26:5; Kavanagh cuts
books in half, gives ct half; gets permission to
keep 2 copies; has sent copy to Brit Museum and
gave 9 copies to P Farrell; Farrell refuses to give
them up; will fight any action by Library, Ja 26,1:2
    NYC Sheriff, under NY Pub Library writ, searches
P Farrell apt for 9 of Kavanagh's home-made books;
friend of Farrell takes books out during search;
Library withdraws writ, F 24,39:4

Fig. 4.1

to published works of arrivals in the United States and Canada; Detroit: Gale, 1981)

Special collections may be devoted to special subjects—for example,
the NYPL's Jewish Division covering religion, history, culture, and
current events; its Arents Collections devoted solely to works about
tobacco and "books in part"; its Dance Collection; and its Map Division. These have special bibliographies and guides.

Newspapers

Old newspapers are invaluable sources for researchers, for obituaries
and, most important, for a social and economic picture of the past.
Most are kept on microfilm and are readily obtained through interlibrary loan if your research library does not have them. The indices to
newspapers are informative in themselves; for instance, the famous
case of the Quinn papers in The New York Public Library in the mid-
1960s was indexed in the *New York Times* as shown in Fig. 4.1.

Patents

Much of patents research is computerized today. Patent diagrams can
be brought to the monitor screen. Patent specifications, abstracts of
patents, patents lists, and related periodicals and books are what you
work with to find if an invention has been patented. The NYPL Patents Collection, for instance, receives publications on patents from the
United States, England, France, Germany, and about 35 other coun-

tries. It has a comprehensive historical collection as well. The two major publications you will use are U.S. Patent Office, *Index of Patents* (1790–   ) and *Manual of Classification.*

Trademark publications can be found for all countries represented by patents. The New York Public Library has a catalog of trademarks registered in the U.S. Patent Office through part of 1947, which has been superseded by *Trademark Register* (1961–64, 1967–   ) and *Trademark Renewal Register* (1964 and 1966). For other special catalogs and files on patents and trademarks, see page 288 of *Guide to the Research Collections of The New York Public Library* (Chicago: ALA, 1975) compiled by Sam P. Williams.

Picture Collections
The Picture Collection at NYPL's Mid-Manhattan Library is used largely by commercial artists who borrow pictures for aid in their artwork and design. For readers seeking illustrations to accompany a book or article, the most important thing to remember is to ask the librarian for the subject, such as "I want a picture of a printing press," not "I want a picture of the process of printing."

The collection has 15,000 subject headings. Culled from books, magazines, newspapers, and other sources, each mounted picture is given a number by which you can look up a bibliographic citation of the publication from which it came. The source catalog holds 19,000 citations.

The collection is divided at the year 1906. Pictures after 1906 are kept by subject heading in vertical files as the main part of the collection. Here, readers may borrow pictures for reproduction purposes or to use in design and artwork (other libraries will photocopy such material). Pictures before that date are kept in vertical files in a special area; they are not loaned, but may be photocopied.

Special collections of postcards depicting places, an alphabetical file of royalty, by country, a personalities file, by name, and a geographic clipping file are also included in the Picture Collection.

Bibliographic Sources
Jessie Croft Ellis, *Index to Illustrations* (Boston: Faxon, 1966)
Isabel Stevenson Munro and Kate M Munro, *Index to Reproductions of European Paintings* (New York: H.W. Wilson, 1956)
Jessie Croft Ellis, *Nature and Its Applications* (over 200,000 selected

references to nature forms and illustrations of nature, as used in
every way; Boston: Faxon, 1949)

Marsha C. Appel, *Illustration Index* (Metuchen, NJ: Scarecrow Press,
1980) and 1977–81 (1984)

Jane Clapp, *Art in Life* (New York: Scarecrow Press, 1959) and
Supplement (1965)

Copyright. When you republish pictures, you should be careful to get
permission from whoever holds the copyright. According to copyright
law, items published with notice of copyright before 1978 are copy-
righted for 28 years and can be renewed for another 28 years. For
photos published after 1978, the copyright duration is for the author's
lifetime plus 50 years. For works made for hire, copyright lasts for 75
years from the date of publication, or 100 years from its creation,
whichever is less. Copyrights made before 1978 but renewed after
1978 are renewable for 47 years.

In this regard the Picture Collection's sources file, to which each
picture is linked by its unique number, is particularly useful. Often,
of course, for pictures from old periodicals and books with no available current address of publisher, permission to publish can be safely
disregarded—not, however, for still flourishing magazines like the *New
Yorker.*

RESEARCHING IN THE PERFORMING ARTS

Theater

You begin your research by thinking of the type of materials you will
be looking at—published works, playscripts, prompt books, clippings,
old newspapers, periodicals, playbills, programs, photographs, letters,
documents. These are all found in a great collection such as NYPL's
Billy Rose Theatre Collection. You may find yourself jumping from
one type of material to another as you compare prompt books with
playscripts, reviews in the clipping file with comments in published
memoirs, or photographs of the stage or movie stills (the NYPL collection has 2 million glossy movie stills). Much of this material is
found by author or subject in the collection's special card catalog.

You will have to consult other library departments because the collections overlap. For instance, typed librettos of musical comedies are

kept in the Billy Rose Theatre Collection but the published librettos are in the Music Division. On the other hand, both published and typed filmscripts are in the Theater Collection. The Berg Collection has letters and scripts of dramatists and actors. Check the other great theatre collections: the Harvard and Yale University Libraries, the Players Club on Gramercy Park, New York City, and the Schubert Archives of New York City. New York University's Tamiment Library has the Archives of Actor's Equity, the American Guild of Variety Artists, and other groups.

Photographs

To find who holds the copyright on photographs, you can use *The Theater World,* an annual pictorial history for the season. (*Screen World* and *Dance World* are helpful resources as well.) The *New York Times* is a good source, because it includes the name of the photographer under the photograph.

Theater Data Base

The Theater Research Data Center at Brooklyn College, in New York City, under the direction of Dr. Irving Brown, is building a data bank of articles, books, theses, films, microfilm, folios—every form of published material on the subject of theater. It is international in scope, with input at present from 14 nations and document centers in Europe and Asia. It may be accessed through the online network system of City University of New York (CUNY). The entries are arranged according to the five major classification headings for theater, and the standard subject headings for theater are used. The system includes a subject index, a document author index, and a content index arranged by geographic location. An annual printed bibliography lists the inputs during the year, beginning with *International Bibliography of the Theater: 1982* (Brooklyn: Theater Research Data Center, 1985).

Theater Sources

Whalan, Marion K. *Performing Arts Research* (a guide to information sources; Detroit: Gale, 1976). This is one of several bibliographies to all aspects and types of materials in the performing arts information guide series issued by the publisher Gale.

Performing Arts Libraries and Museums of the World, 3rd ed. (Paris: Centre National de la Recherche Scientifique, 1984).

Music

A large portion of music research parts company with the usual sort of research in published and unpublished sources—that is, the study of musical scores to establish either the composer or the latest and best score. This is meticulous work that requires gathering of bits of information from manuscript sources, scores, and contemporary accounts, often over the course of a researcher's lifetime before a pattern is found.

An international joint effort has been made to control information on music written before 1800, with the RISM (Repertoire International des Sources Musicales/International Inventory of Musical Sources) *Einzeldrucke vor 1800* (Kassel: Barenreiter; London: Basel Tours), published in a multivolumed set.

RISM is establishing a data bank for musical manuscripts before 1800. The system will have an added advantage: the musical beginnings to pieces can be fed into the data bank, which facilitates identification.

A major difficulty with using catalogs to music collections is the variety of ways in which scores are cataloged. In the United States, alone, the *conventional title* is used.

The great music collections are in the Oesterreichisches Nationalbibliothek and the Gesellschaft für Musikfreunde in Vienna. Italy has several good libraries. (See, RISM's *Director of Music Research Libraries:* vol. 1, Canada and the United States; vol. 2, Thirteen European countries; vol. 3, Spain, France, Italy, Portugal; vol. 4, Australia, Israel, Japan, New Zealand.)

Bibliographic Sources

Vincent Druckles, *Music Reference and Research Materials,* 3rd ed. (New York: Free Press, 1974)

Ruth T. Watanabe, *Introduction to Music Research* (Englewood Cliffs, NJ: Prentice-Hall, 1967)

Anna Harriett Heyer, *Historical Sets, Collected Editions, and Monuments of Music* (a guide to their contents), 3rd ed. (Chicago: ALA, 1980) in 2 vols. (It lists the publications and gives bibliographic information and list of contents.)

Dance

To approach a unique collection in a research library, you should read the description of its resources in the library's Guide before using the collection. In the case of the NYPL's Dance Collection at the Performing Arts Research Center, for example, you should read the detailed description in the *Guide to the Research Collections of the New York Public Library,* compiled by Sam Williams (Chicago: ALA, 1975) p. 150–56. It tells you that the Dance Collection includes ethnic, primitive, folk and modern dance, ballet, and social forms as various as the minuet and cha-cha; that pictorial material forms the major part of the collection; and that it has tens of thousands of prints, librettos, stage designs, programs, and other material and thousands of reels of motion picture film. The Library's most recently published brochures and reports will provide the latest information. Readers at the collection are often dancers seeking to recreate dances from still photographs, as Nureyev recreated Nijinsky's "The Afternoon of a Faun" (1912) from the Library's collection of Nijinsky photographs.

The Dance Collection *Dictionary Catalog,* therefore, is an amalgam of special files organized by dance steps, titles of dances, dance iconography, and other systems, and the regular book-catalog form of entry. The entries are arranged under established headings of the form of the material: books and periodical articles, visual material, music, and audio material. You will find that the scope is broad; for instance, entries for individual titles cover professional performances and note the first performance, the first performance in the United States, the first performance in New York, the first performance by a major company other than the original, and also performances with new or revised staging or choreography.

MEDICAL LIBRARIES

You cannot afford to overlook other specialized libraries in doing research. For instance the great collection of the New York Academy of Medicine Library (2 East 103 St., New York, New York) is open to the public. Here you can find almost every publication on medicine and related subjects, such as psychoanalysis, pharmacy, foods, and cookery. The library collects rare books and incunabula on medicine, minutes of medical societies, portraits of medical men, and many other materials. It collects all editions of medical works in all languages. Having all editions in all languages is important to the researcher; for example, William Harvey wrote in Latin, but translations of his works include commentaries and additional material. The library currently receives 4,000 serial titles and has a great collection of old medical periodicals in all languages.

You can find reports on the diseases of well-known and unknown people, correspondence of medical men from all over the world, from modern to ancient times, a portrait catalog of medical people, and a catalog of illustrations analyzed by the librarians from publications on the history of medicine. These sources are useful for researchers in other fields. Those who picture medical libraries as containing mainly indices and abstracts of medical articles, much of it online, will be surprised to learn that the library collects works of history comprehensively, because medicine must be studied in relation to the world around it.

LAW

To begin research in U.S. law, you should turn first to *Shepard's Citations,* to determine the current status of your primary legal source (i.e., a decision, statute, or an administrative regulation or ruling). This research step is essential because of the doctrine of precedent and *stare decisis,* and because, strictly speaking, decisions and statutes remain in effect, regardless of their age, unless and until they are reversed, overruled, or, in the case of statutes, repealed or judicially declared void.

Shepard's citator system comprises state units, regional units, federal units, and specialized citator units. Many nations have equivalent citator systems.

Major research libraries carry the laws of all nations and of all state or regional units. You can differentiate between slip laws and consolidated laws or revised statutes. Slip laws are the laws issued by a legislature during the year and are bound together in order of issue. To find a slip law, you must know the year it was passed. Consolidated laws are the laws in force, brought together in a uniform set of volumes with indices. In earlier years they were called revised statutes. You can also use these consolidated laws to find laws that are no longer in force, because under the wording of the law or statute there is a list of citations of the laws from which it was derived. You then find the earlier law by year in the slip laws. For instance, the *United States Code* may refer to an historical precedent as 12Stat.146. This earlier law is found in *The United States Statutes,* vol. 12, p. 146.

If you are preparing your own case, you should be familiar with the volumes of *Federal Procedure* (Rochester, NY: Lawyers Cooperative Publishing Co), which is arranged alphabetically and explains the procedure for bringing your case to federal criminal and civil courts and administrative boards. Along with these volumes, you need *Federal Procedural Forms,* by the same publisher.

The best access to case law, by subject, is *West's Federal Practice Digests.* There are four editions, each covering a different time period.

Finally, law libraries keep sample briefs on file, useful for someone who needs a model to prepare a brief on a certain subject for a certain court.

Law libraries are open to the public in some countries, such as England. In the United States they are usually private. In New York City, however, the U.S. Court of Appeals Library on the 25th floor of the U.S. Courthouse, Foley Square, admits public researchers, although technically it is for the court staff. The New York Public Library issues METRO cards to readers to visit university law libraries in the New York City area for legal publications that the public library does not carry.

GENERAL RULES FOR WHEN TO USE WHAT

1. When doing research on a general topic, break it down into smaller topics, which you can then relate better to the reference guides, the catalog subject entries, and bibliographies.
2. For historical research, begin by looking under subject headings in the library catalogs.
3. For current research, begin by looking in the periodical indices in your subject field.
4. When researching a project for a long period, vary your search from events to biographies to theory, to avoid becoming stale. This also gives you fresh ideas by showing you former sources in the light of a new approach.
5. Research, by its nature, requires you to redefine your goals at

intervals. This must be done at the right times; otherwise, you waste your time and, perhaps, lose your way.

6. Research tools, such as online information systems, which are subsidiary to the catalog must be regarded as mere helpmeets. The Library catalog and accompanying indices to the collection not in the catalog are your fundamental tools. You work with the collection and get your inspiration and pleasure from it. Online systems and periodical indices are patterned by others, but your research must be unique as you develop your own pattern.

7. Remember the variety of forms in which you may find your material. Special pamphlet collections, manuscript collections, photograph, and print collections may help you pursue your subject. Always keep an eye peeled for book catalogs to these special collections.

8. Remember the *National Union Catalog of Books and Pamphlets,* the *Union List of Serials,* and other bibliographic location guides. Extend the walls of your research library to encompass the North American continent through the services of interlibrary loan.

9. Researchers in the humanities should rely first on book bibliographies; in the social sciences and the sciences, you should rely first on periodical indices and abstracts.

10. Always use the same notebooks in your research. Scraps of paper and occasional notebooks will most likely be lost. Also, it helps to keep a record near you of what you have seen. Many researchers have begun to study the same book twice. And keep a full bibliographical record of your sources, and that means *page numbers* as well. Trying to relocate a source can be mental torture.

WHEN TO USE OTHER LIBRARIES

Avoid beginning research in a small library; you will just be discouraged prematurely. Pack up and go to Washington, New York, or Boston. If you use a major university library, the resources of the large research libraries will be available to you through interlibrary loan.

If you are researching in medicine, you must use a medical library because general research libraries do not collect in the field. In America the researcher in law can find fundamental legal information—law, cases, forms guides, and legal periodicals (to which he uses the *Index to Legal Periodicals*)—but study beyond the superficial requires permission to use one of the private law libraries, which can be difficult to obtain.

If researching in a specialized subject, you should go directly to the collection that appears to have the most material; for instance, when studying the American Revolutionary War in New York State you would research in the manuscript collections in the New-York Historical Society; later you would visit the New York State Library in Albany and the American Antiquarian Society in Worcester, Massachusetts. The New York Public Library also has strong early American collections. First, of course, you would have read the major published works on the subject, which you should be able to obtain in a medium-sized city library. Once a general understanding is formed, a deeper knowledge can be obtained only by studying the primary materials. At this point, your research begins.

THE MICROFORM PROBLEM—HOW TO DEAL WITH IT

The polluted air of the industrialized era has turned library materials to sawdust. A rescue operation called "Conservation" treated old paper with chemicals to hold it together until it could be microfilmed. Libraries pooled their resources and funds in microform projects such as the National Gazettes on Microform, which involved libraries internationally.

Aside from the necessity of preservation, library administrators became worried about shelf space. They saw microform as an answer to space problems. They began buying microfilm runs of periodical sets and throwing out the bound copies, regardless of the perfect state of the paper. Current periodicals were no longer bound, but purchased in microfilm reels. Government publications, particularly the all-important U.S. congressional hearings were purchased on microfiches; indices to them were purchased from the same company, thus obviating the need to enter them into the library catalog. The administrators explained that this saved money in bindery expenses and cataloging time.

Because administrators are not researchers they could not have understood the difficulty of locating materials, especially congressional hearings, in the library catalogs. This difficulty is increased when items in the collection are not cataloged; indeed, it throws the researcher on the mercy of the librarian for information on where such items may be found and for guidance through the intricate procedure of locating the microfiche copy.

Also, administrators are not aware of the impracticality of researching with microform when indices (which are somewhere else on the reel or on another fiche) have to be constantly consulted, necessitating frequent changing of reels or fiche on the reading machine. With frequent use, microform becomes scratched, sometimes illegible. Although desperate attempts are being made to improve microform readers, they cause great discomfort to the reader compelled to sit at them for any length of time. Microform also decays—in some instances it deteriorates faster than paper. Regarding storage, it can fit into a smaller space than a book, but it can be lost or stolen more easily. And if it has not been cataloged, its loss will not be known unless some attempt is made to record its presence in the library's collection.

Not being researchers, library administrators also have no idea of the eye strain experienced by researchers when reading microform. But because "the microform solution" (with its accompanying expense to libraries and bonanza to microform companies) has been widely adopted, researchers must look to their own defenses.

The use of microfilm for spot references can be helpful in research libraries, as the films are made available quickly and modern machines can roll the film speedily, thus avoiding the tiresome cranking of the old reading machines. But for reading at length, the researcher should avoid the microforms if possible. Here are some tips on how this can be done:

1. For very important papers, research libraries keep two copies: one on microform and one in paper. The microform is given to students and casual researchers. For those reading at length in these papers, the paper copy can be located. The New York Public Library Research Libraries, for example, make the U.S. congressional set of reports and documents available in microprint cards, but it also preserves the bound volumes.

2. There may be libraries in the same city that still keep the pamphlets and periodicals on paper that your major research library has converted to microform. You can either arrange to use that library or ask for the materials through interlibrary loan.

3. If the volumes can be found only in microform, the reader can have them reproduced in xerox pages (at a high cost) and take them

home to read. The clearinghouse for *Dissertations Abstracts* in Ann Arbor, Michigan, provides researchers with either microfilm or xerox volume of the dissertation requested.

4. If back issues of periodicals are on microfilm, the reader may procure back issues in paper from the publisher.

Admittedly these strategies cause delay and inconvenience, but researchers may wish to adopt them to save themselves from eye strain.

Appendix: World's Major Research Libraries and Methods of Approach

In this section are brief summaries of some of the world's major research libraries and the different methods of searching required in each. It is always advisable to confirm hours and location of any special divisions before a visit.

THE NEW YORK PUBLIC LIBRARY

Central Research Library

42nd St. and Fifth Ave., New York, NY 10018
Hours: Mon.–Sat.
Main Reading Room: Open: 10 A.M.–8:45 P.M., Mon.–Wed.
            10 A.M.–5:45 P.M., Thurs.–Sat.
Other divisions have different hours.
The 43rd Street *Annex* off Tenth Avenue is open, 9 A.M.–4:45 P.M., Mon.–Sat.

Admission. No card or admission ticket is required, except for the Special Collections, for which you can obtain a pass from the Special Collections Admissions Office.

Layout. The New York Public Library provides a good example of how research libraries are divided into subject divisions. All libraries have a central catalog room and central reading room. Special divisions are in the same building or other buildings either in the next block or miles away. Sometimes the special divisions have direct communication with the central reading room by which you can request books from the special divisions to read in the central reading room. In other cases, the special divisions are completely separated from the central reading room, and you must go to those divisions to read their books.

The front entrance to NYPL's Central Research Library is from Fifth Avenue. Exhibit halls encompass the central portion of the ground floor. Down the hallway to your left are the Periodicals Section (Room 108), where you can read current periodicals in the humanities and of a general nature. ("Current" means periodicals issued within the present year.) Down the hallway on your right are the Science and Technology Research Center (Room 121). Current issues of periodicals on scientific and technological subjects are found there, not in the Periodicals Section. For instance, the *Women's Wear Daily* is kept here.

The Map Division is across the hallway (Room 119).

On this right side of the building is an elevator, as well as a marble stairway; also stairs lead from either side of the front foyer. Taking the elevator to the second floor, you can walk directly into the Economic and Public Affairs Division (Room 228). This division gives you access to publications in the social sciences, business, finance, and government. Current issues of periodicals in these subjects are found here as well.

Proceeding down the second floor hallway you will find a central corridor branching off at a right angle. Down this corridor is the Slavonic Division (Room 217) for literature, including periodicals, in the Slavonic languages, and the Oriental Division (Room 219) for literature, including periodicals, in the Oriental languages.

At the far end of the main hallway are the Administrative Offices of the Library and The Research Libraries.

Proceeding up the stairway to the third floor you will encounter, leading off from the center of the hallway, the General Research Division (Room 315), where the central catalog room is located; beyond this are the two-part central or Main Reading Room. In Room 315 the computer and book catalogs for all the works in The Research Libraries are kept, including those of the special divisions. Here, also, are research librarians ready to help you locate materials and file request slips for publications.

Beyond this outer room, two reading halls, divided by an enclosure, provide you with many reading tables and ready reference books lining the shelves. At the center enclosure are light indicators that light up indicator numbers when requested books are brought up from the books stacks below.

In the reading room to the right (the North Hall, as distinct from the reading room on the left, which is called the South Hall) is an area for reading microforms at microform machines. This is the Microforms Division (Room 315M). At the end of the North Hall is the U.S. History, Local History and Genealogy Division (Room 315N). The histories of countries, cities, and smaller incorporations are kept here with the genealogical publications, whereas the histories of nations are located in the General Research Division.

Passing back through the central catalog room to the third floor hallway you will find on your right the Wallach Division of Art, Prints and Photographs (Room 313). The Art Room for researchers in the fine arts is open without restriction like the subject divisions we have mentioned, but the Print and Photographic Collections (Room 308) further down the hall require a special reader's pass from the Special Collections Office (Room 316).

Along the hallway in the other direction is the Pforzheimer Collection "Shelley and His Circle" devoted to works of the English Romantic poets (Room 319) and, across the hall from it, the Berg Collection of rare books and manuscripts in English and American literature. Around the bend in the hallway is the Arents Collections of works on tobacco and books in parts (Room 324). Currently (1987), users of Manuscript and Archives and Rare Book Room materials are directed to this room. All of these collections require the special reader's pass.

Taking the elevator down to the ground floor, you will come across the Jewish Division (Room 84) near the 42nd Street entrance. The Jewish Division has materials relating to the Jewish culture and religion, including periodicals and publications in microform.

Performing Arts Research Center

To reach the Music Division, the Billy Rose Theatre Collection, the Rodgers and Hammerstein Archives of Recorded Sound, and the Dance Collection, you take a 104 bus on the opposite side of 42nd Street, going west for about 20 minutes to the Lincoln Center complex at Broadway and 65th Street. Between the Opera House and the Vivian Beaumont Theater is an entrance to the Library & Museum of the

Performing Arts. On the first two floors are the Branch Libraries units. On the third floor are the above-mentioned collections of the NYPL Research Libraries' Performing Arts Research Center.

Annex

If you wish to see the Newspaper Collection and the Patents (and Trademarks) Collection, you take a 105 bus across the street from the 42nd Street entrance, going west for about 10 minutes to Tenth Avenue on 42nd Street. Walking one block to West 43rd Street and then west for a quarter-block to the New York Public Library Annex, you will find newspapers from cities around the world and gain quick access to information on patents worldwide. Publications that have been crowded out of the central building are also kept in this annex; for instance, books on religion are shelved here.

Schomburg Center for Research in Black Culture

This collection of publications and manuscripts related to black culture is housed in a modern research library building at Lenox Avenue and 135th Street. On leaving the central building, you would go to the Times Square subway station and take the uptown No. 2 train of the IRT Seventh Avenue express line. This takes you directly to the Schomburg Center at the 135th Street stop.

The center comprises several sections, each dedicated to the acquisition of the format of materials it represents, such as General Research and Reference, Rare Books, Manuscripts and Archives, Moving Images and Recorded Sound, Arts and Artifacts, Photographs and Prints, and so on.

Items in the NYPL catalogs with call numbers beginning with ''Sc'' are in the Schomburg Center.

Connections with the Main Reading Room

Rather than travel to the annex to read a book, you may request it through the Information Desk in Room 315. The requested book will arrive in two days and be put under your name on the reserve shelves, where it will remain for a week.

You may request publications (except for current periodicals) from the Economic and Public Affairs Division in Room 315 when both are open at the same time.

Publications in all other special divisions you must request and read in those divisions. Note carefully the hours when the special divisions are open, because they may differ from the hours of the Main Reading Room and from each other.

Mid-Manhattan Library

The Mid-Manhattan Library is the main library of the NYPL Branch Libraries. Located on Fifth Avenue and 40th Street across from the Central Research Library, it has both circulating and reference books. For periodicals and books that The Research Libraries do not have, you should check in the book *Catalog* of the *Branch Libraries* to see if they are available for you to borrow or read at the Mid-Manhattan Library or at other branches. The Research Libraries, for example, do not collect books on medicine, but the Mid-Manhattan Library keeps such books in its Science Department. Also, if periodicals you want are in use at The Research Libraries, you may find them at Mid-Manhattan.

HARVARD UNIVERSITY LIBRARY

Harvard University, Cambridge, MA (branches in other locations, e.g., Boston, Washington, DC, Florence, Italy)

Admission. If you are not from Harvard, write to the librarian to obtain permission to use the library.

Layout. The library comprises more than 10 million volumes and more than 100 libraries, many of which service the particular professional school to which they are attached; thus, they tend to be subject-specialty libraries—for business, law, medicine, education, or divinity, for example. Others are truly specialized libraries—those for the fine arts, music, rare books and manuscripts, the physical, applied, and biological sciences, among others. Also within these libraries are specialized collections. The main research library is the Widener Library in the center of the campus; it serves the social sciences and humanities. The visitor should seek information on the research collections at

Harvard from the numerous publications available and the Widener reference staff. Most Harvard libraries allow university-affiliated users to borrow materials. As in most university libraries, the reader can retrieve his or her books directly from the stacks.

Catalogs. Every Harvard Library or specialized collection has its own catalog. The Union Catalog, a card catalog by author that was closed off in 1977, is located on the main floor of the Widener Library and contains the majority of Harvard's earlier holdings. For the period from 1977 to date, you can use the Distributable Union Catalog (DUC) in microfiche, which covers most of the Harvard libraries and can be found in 130 locations. It is divided into an author-title section, a subject section, a medical subject section, and a monthly author-title supplement. Not listed in the DUC, but found in individual library catalogs, are works in Arabic, Chinese, Japanese, Korean, other languages of East Asia, older books in Hebrew and Yiddish, manuscripts, archival materials, maps, sound recordings, and visual materials.

Background. Founded in 1638, it is the oldest library in the United States and the largest university library in the world.

BRITISH LIBRARY (ENGLAND)

Reference Division, The British Museum, Great Russell St.,
London WCLB 3DG (Tel: 01-636-1544)
Hours: Mon., Fri., Sat. 9 A.M.–5 P.M.
        Tues., Wed., Thurs. 9 A.M.–9 P.M.
        Closed for the week following the last complete week in October,
        and on Sundays and major holidays.

Admission. Free, but you must obtain a reader's ticket with a letter of reference from a professor or consulate official.

Layout. The Department of Printed Books on the ground floor comprises the central reading halls and contains books and periodicals on all subjects except current science and technology, and in all but the Oriental languages. Many of its books are kept in the Annex at Woolwich. In other rooms, you will find the Official Publications Library, housing the largest collection in Europe of official papers of all periods and countries and publications of intergovernmental bodies; the Map Library; the Music Library; the Department of Oriental Manuscripts and Printed Books, covering the literature of the Orient and North Africa; the Department of Manuscripts, comprising books and documents of every kind in manuscript (including maps and music) in European languages from the classical period to the present (for which you require a special pass).

The Science Reference Library comprises (1) the Bayswater Branch Building, which concentrates on the life sciences including medical science and scientific publications in Slavonic and Oriental languages, and (2) the Holborn Branch Building, which includes the Patent Office Library and most of the chemical and physical sciences and technologies. No admissions ticket is required to enter the Science Library.

The Newspaper Library at Colindale, North London, contains newspapers published after 1800, from all countries, and British provincial papers published before 1800.

The library also has photoreproduction facilities.

Catalogs. The General Catalogue is contained in looseleaf volumes shelved at the center of the Reading Room. It contains entries for works received in the Department of Printed Books through 1970, which are arranged in columns by main entry, with supplementary slips for works added to the collections from 1956 to 1970 and mounted beside the columns from 1975. A published Subject Index to the General Catalogue covers accessions from 1861 to 1960, in book form, with acquisitions from 1961 in microform cassettes. For the other departments you should use the catalogs particular to them.

Requesting Books. When you fill out call slips and leave them at the central desk, the books are brought to the seat number you have written on the call slip. Delivery can take more than an hour, or even two days if the book is at the Woolwich Annex; in this case it is put on the reserve shelves under your name. (The British Library provides a free pamphlet for readers, ''No. 7, How to Use the Catalogues.'')

You must return your books to the central desk and retrieve your request slip.

To avoid waiting for books to be delivered, you may post request slips to the library up to 24 hours in advance. The books are kept on reserve for you.

Background. The library's nucleus consists of the collection of books and manuscripts brought together on the foundation of the British Museum in 1753. The old Royal Library was given to the British Museum in 1757, and the right to a deposit copy of every book published in the United Kingdom was transferred with it. Foreign material is obtained by purchase or exchange from most countries. The total number of books exceeds 10 million.

Useful Guides.

Foster, Janet and Julia Sheppard, *British Archives: a Guide to Archive Resources in the United Kingdom* (Detroit: Gale, 1982)

Bond, Maurice F., *Guide to the Records of Parliament* (London: HMSO: 1971)

Cox, Jane and Timothy Padfield, *Tracing Your Ancestors in the Public Record Office* (London: HMSO, 1983)

BIBLIOTHÈQUE NATIONALE (FRANCE)

58 rue Richelieu, 75084 Paris Cedex 02 (Tel: 261-82-83)
Hours: Mon.–Sat., 9 A.M.–6P.M.
    Closed second and third weeks after Easter.

Admission. You need a letter from a university official or your cultural attaché certifying your need to use the library. You pay a fee for an identification card and provide two full-face photographs, one of which is attached to your card.

Layout. The Central Reading Room, on the ground floor, contains books and publications for general research. Specialized departments in the building are maps and plans, stamps and photographs, manuscripts, coins and medals and antiques, music, national record library and audiovisual aids, and theater arts. The Bibliothèque de l'Arsenal (1 rue de Sully, 75004 Paris) specializing in literature and theater, the Bibliothèque du Conservatoire, Nationale Superieure de Musique (114 rue de Madrid, 75008 Paris) and the Bibliothèque-Musée de l'Opèra (Place Charles Garnier, 75009 Paris) are attached to it. In the central building the catalog room *(salle des catalogues)* is reached from the Central Reading Room down a flight of stairs. It is a large room with a smaller adjoining periodicals room where reference librarians are stationed.

Catalogs. The *Catalogue général des libres imprimés* comprises more than 200 volumes arranged by author from A (published in 1897) through V (published in 1969). The date on which each volume was printed is on the cover, so that you know you cannot expect to find a publication published after that date in that volume. In this case, you turn to four other catalogs: (1) If the work is by an author whose name falls between VIB and Z, and was published before 1882, consult the card catalog by authors of acquisitions prior to 1882. (2) If the work was acquired between 1882 and 1935, but too late to be included in the proper volume in the *Catalogue général,* it can be found in the sheaf catalogs with red and white backs. (3) If the work was received between 1936 and 1959, it can be found in the card catalog of acquisitions between 1936 and 1939; if received between 1960 and 1969, it can be found in the card catalog of acquisitions 1960–69; if received between 1970 and the present date, it can be found in the card catalog for acquisitions since 1970. (4) Works between 1960 and 1964 can be found in the book *Catalogue general, auteurs et anonymes,* and in the card catalog 1960–69. For anonymous or corporate authorship (public or private), look in the *Catalogue général, auteurs et anonymes* or in the special card catalogs for acquisitions from 1950 and 1960 to 1969 and 1970 plus.

Subject catalogs include the following:

1. 1882–94 in bound indices.
2. 1894–1925 collections in mobile bindings with white and green backs.
3. 1925–35 collections bound in black cloth.
4. 1935–59 in card catalogs.
5. Since 1960 in card catalogs, or for the period 1960–64, in the *Catalogue général.*

For recent books, when you know the year of publication, look in the *Bibliographie de la France,* which gives the Bibliothèque Nationale call number with the bibliographic description.

Requesting Books. You fill out a request slip with your seat number and hand it in to the library clerk in the central reading room. The books are delivered to your seat. Ten thousand reference works are available on the open shelves of the reading room, and a card index to them is located at the entrance.

Background. The Bibliothèque du Roi began in the age of Charlemagne. It was housed first in the Louvre by Charles V, was broken up and reestablished at Fontainebleau in 1544, became a *dépôt légal,* was rehoused in the rue Vivienne in the age of Louis XIV, and grew rapidly in its present location until the Revolution. The new National Assembly then transformed it by requiring that it absorb all Parisian ecclesiastical libraries and aristocratic *émigré* libraries; by 1794 it had grown fivefold in five years.

Useful Guides.

France, Ministère de l'éducation nationale, *Catalogue général des manuscripts des bibliothèques publiques de France* (Paris: 1885– 1965), 55 vols. in 62

Librairies and Archives in France; a Handbook, ed. Erwin K. Welsch (Pittsburgh: Council for European Studies, 1973)

STATE V. I. LENIN LIBRARY OF THE USSR

101000 Moscow, Prospekt Kalinina, 3 (Tel: 202-57-90)
Hours: 9 A.M.–10 P.M. every day, including Sun. Closed on major holidays.

Admission. The library can be used only by students pursuing advanced degrees or university-trained researchers. (Workers use the public libraries.) To obtain a reader's ticket, you should have an official letter verifying the purpose of your research, your passport, and photographs of yourself. You must go to the main reading room on the second floor of the new building.

Layout. All of the departments are contained in the same complex of the old building and the new building adjoining it. There are 22 reading rooms with 2230 seats. The main reading halls in both buildings are found on the second floor. There is an annex in Khimki.

Catalogs. Each reading room covers a special subject and has its unique catalog. The main catalog room is on the second floor of the new building. There are 22 different catalogs for books, most of them alphabetical author catalogs, but some classified by subject or by geographic location. There are separate catalogs for periodicals, newspapers, books, and dissertations, and catalogs organized by languages (one alphabetical catalog of Russian-language books, one for Ukrainian books, one for books in the Latin alphabet, one for books in the languages of the people's democracies of Asia). Subject catalogs for scientific disciplines are more detailed in the new building, whereas language and literature catalogs are more detailed in the special reading rooms of the old building.

Material not represented in either the official (for staff only) or public catalogs is kept in a special catalog, unavailable for consultation. Material such as obsolete books, pornography, foreign works unfriendly to the Soviet Union, and works of the "enemies of the people" (i.e., Beria, Bukharin, Radek, Trotsky) is confined to the limbo, or *spetsfond,* of the library.

Reproduction is done by photostat only.

Russian librarians are subject specialists and know the collection in their subject field.

Background. Founded in 1862 as Rumyantsev Library and reorganized in 1925, the library now has more than 28 million books, periodicals, and serials, and complete files of newspapers in all 91 national languages and 156 foreign languages.

Useful Guides.

Patrick K. Grimstead, *Archives and Manuscript Repositories in the U.S.S.R.: Moscow and Leningrad* (Princeton, N.J.: Princeton University Press, 1972), and *Supplement I Bibliographical Archives* (Switzerland: Inter-Documentation, 1976)

Patricia K. Grimstead, *Archives and Manuscript Repositories in the U.S.S.R. Estonia, Latvia, Lithuania and Belorussia* (Princeton, N.J.: Princeton University Press, 1981)

SALTYKOV-SCHCHEDRIN STATE PUBLIC LIBRARY

SADOVAYA U1, 18, (Leningrad) D-69

Hours: open to all, including children of school age, from 9 A.M.–11 P.M.

This library was formed from the Imperial Public Library and has been a depository from 1811, amassing a rich collection. Not only does it provide excellent and detailed reference service, its Bibliographics Division issues many annotated selected bibliographies annually.

NATIONAL LIBRARY OF CHINA

Beijing, 39 Baishi qiao Street, People's Republic of China (tel: 662972)
Hours: Mon.–Fri. 8 A.M. to 8 P.M.; Sun. 8 A.M. to 4 P.M.; closed Sat.

History. Founded as the Capital Library of Peking in 1910, and formally opened to the public in 1912, the National Library's collection incorporates collections formed as far back as 700 years: the Imperial Libraries of the Southern Song Dynasty (1127–1279), the Ming Dynasty (1368–1644), and other prominent collections.

Admission. There are no restrictions. Borrowing privileges are granted to individuals and institutions.

Layout. There are 15 reading rooms, some with seating capacity for 700.

Holdings. The library has 11 million volumes including more than 5 million books (60 percent in Chinese; 40 percent in foreign languages), 4 million bound volumes of periodicals (20 percent in Chinese), 3600 newspaper titles (50 percent in Chinese), and 580,000 volumes of rare early printed works and rare revolutionary documents and manuscripts. The library is a depository for all publications issued in China; publishing houses must send it three copies of every title. It has exchange agreements with about 2000 institutions in 120 countries. It collects books in the 24 national languages of the People's Republic, and English is the most frequently represented foreign language, followed by Russian, Japanese, French, German, and 109 other foreign languages.

Catalogs. Up to 1979, Chinese titles and authors are in the traditional arrangement by number of strokes and their order. Since 1979 Chinese titles and authors have been arranged in alphabetical sequence according to the Pinyin Chinese Phonetic System. The library introduced a new Chinese Classification Scheme in January 1975. (It provides 3000 libraries in China with centralized cataloging cards for new books in Chinese and foreign languages.)

Useful Guide.

John T. Ma, *Chinese Collections in Western Europe; Survey of their Technical and Readers' Service* (Zug. Switz.: Inter Documentation, 1985). (Notes the availability of photographic services.)

NATIONAL DIET LIBRARY (JAPAN)

1-10-1 Nagata-cho, Chiyoda-ku, Tokyo 100 (Tel: 581-2331,2341)

Hours: Mon.–Sat. 9:30 A.M.–5 P.M. (Book delivery service stops at 4 P.M.)

Special Rooms: General Study Room Mon.–Fri., 9:30 A.M.–8 P.M. (for long-range study). Statutes and parliamentary documents room, 9:30 A.M.–8 P.M. Music Library, 1 P.M.–5 P.M.

Closed Sundays, national holidays, Wednesday of the fourth week of every month, and Dec. 28–Jan. 4.

Admission. Admission is free but restricted to readers 20 years of age and older. You obtain a reader's badge and reader's slips (Fig. A.1) at the reader's gate. The slips serve as passes to the reading room: green for the General Reading Rooms 1 and 2, black for other reading rooms, including the Newspaper Reading Room, the Science and Technology Materials Rooms, and the Statutes and Parliamentary Documents Room, and red for the General Study Room.

Layout. The first floor includes the catalogs. On the second floor are the Central Reading Room (382 seats), General Reference Room (76 seats), Newspaper Reading Room (97 seats), UN and Government Materials Room (12 seats), and Music Library (14 seats). The third floor includes a second Central Reading Room (194 seats), the General Study Room (112 seats), the Asian and African Materials Room (32 seats), the Library Science Materials Room (32 seats), the Newspaper Clippings Room (24 seats), Rare Book Reading Room (12 seats), Modern Political History Materials Room (4 seats), and the Shidehara Peace Library (2 seats). On the fourth floor are the Science and Technology Materials Reading Room (59 seats), Constitutional Materials Room (17 seats), and Map Room (10 seats). The fifth floor holds the Statutes and Parliamentary Documents Room (44 seats).

There is a photocopying service.

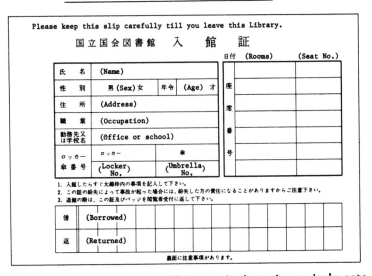

National Diet Library Reader's Slip

Please keep this slip carefully till you leave this Library.

国 立 国 会 図 書 館 　 入 　 館 　 証

1. This reader's slip should be received at the reader's gate.
2. The number on the slip is at the same time the number of the seat assigned to the reader in the reading room.
3. When no seat number is given on the slip, the reader may go to any seat.

Fig. A.1

Requesting Books. Because it is basically a closed-stack library, you must file call slips at the central circulation counter (Fig. A.2). As a foreigner, you should write your name in block letters, or preferably in *katakana.* When the books or journals arrive from the stacks, you will be paged. Show your reader's slip and have the "borrowed" column rubber-stamped. When finished, you return the materials to the counter that received them from the stacks and have the "returned" column of your reader's slip rubber-stamped. Your badges and slips are returned to the officer at the readers' gate. You cannot take books out of the library.

Background. The National Diet Library inherited the collection of the Japanese Imperial Library, which was founded as the sole national

National Diet Library Call Slip

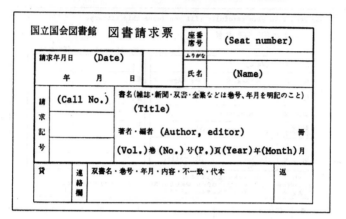

Fig. A.2

library at the beginning of the Meiji era (1867). Since its founding in 1948, it has acted as Japan's legal deposit library.

U.S. LIBRARY OF CONGRESS

Washington, DC 20540 (Tel: 202-287-5000)
Hours: General Reading Rooms: 8:30 A.M.–9:30 P.M., Mon.–Fri.; 8:30 A.M.–5 P.M. on Sat.; and 1 P.M.–5 P.M. on Sun.

The largest library in the United States, the Library of Congress serves primarily congresspersons but is open to the general public over high school age. No reading ticket is required. The library operates like The New York Public Library. Readers fill out request slips for books and periodicals.

Reading Rooms. There are two general reading rooms: the Main Reading Room on the first floor of the Thomas Jefferson Building, and the Thomas Jefferson Reading Room on the fifth floor of the John Adams Building (nearby, between Second and Third Streets, S.E.). Books from the general collections may be requested in either of these rooms, but you should use the reading room in the building that houses the collections you want to consult. There are 20 specialized reading rooms, many of them covering the subjects of the special divisions of The New York Public Library. Unlike The New York Public Library, however, the Library of Congress has a Law Library; this is one of the most comprehensive collections of legal materials ever developed, in all languages and covering all legal systems, both ancient and modern. You can find reference assistance and access to relevant Law Library collections through the Anglo-American Reading Room on the second floor of the Jefferson Building and in international and foreign law through the European, Far Eastern, Hispanic, and Near Eastern and African Law Divisions. There is a National Library Service for the Blind and Handicapped at 1291 Taylor Street, N.W. (The Library for the Blind and Physically Handicapped of The New York Public Library [at the corner of Spring and Avenue of the Americas] is part of the Branch Libraries system.)

In addition are the U.S. Copyright Office and the Congressional Research Service.

The Copyright Office of the Library of Congress (James Madison Memorial Building, 101 Independence Avenue, S.E., Washington, DC 20559) is open to the public from 8:30 A.M. to 5 P.M. Monday through Friday (except for legal holidays). The various records freely available to the public include an extensive card catalog, an automated catalog containing records from 1978 forward, record books, and microfilm records of assignments and related documents. Other records, including correspondence file and deposit copies, are not open to the public for searching. They may be inspected, however, on request and a payment of a $10-per-hour search fee.

The Congressional Research Service does searches only for members of Congress (about a half-million searches a year). Its Selective Dissemination of Information service provides congressional patrons with photocopies of the text of citations available in an online data base. It uses microcomputer and telecommunications technology in its internal operations. The public's access is limited to reading *CRS Review,* which features current topics of major legislative interest in magazine format, and *CRS Studies in the Public Domain,* a semiannual listing of all the CRS research products that have been printed by the Congress and are available as committee prints, House or Senate documents or reports, or insertions in the *Congressional Record.*

Catalogs. The Main Catalog (beginning in the Main Reading Room and extending into the adjoining rooms and corridor) contains printed author, title, and subject cards interfiled into a single alphabetical sequence. (In the Thomas Jefferson Reading Room you have to use printed book catalogs adjacent to the reading room). At the end of the card catalog is the Computer Catalog Center, which provides online information on English-language books cataloged from 1968 to the present and on books in most other Western languages added since 1973. The catalogs in the special reading rooms, especially those of the Rare Book and Special Collections Reading Room, also supplement the general catalogs.

A separate catalog of serials adjoins the Main Catalog, and a list of the most frequently used periodicals, with call numbers included, is available at the Central and the Reference desks. There is also a serials catalog in the Science Reading Room, adjacent to the Thomas Jefferson Reading Room. Before visiting The Library of Congress you can check its holdings in its printed book catalogs or in the NUC (see p. 57) found in other research libraries.

The Library's SCORPIO computer system gives you access to cataloging and other information in four separate data bases: (1) the Computerized Catalog for books accessioned after 1968, (2) the Bibliographic Citation File, for periodical articles and government publications on public policy subjects for the current year and the two previous years, (3) the Legislative Files, for public bills and resolutions introduced into Congress for the current and the two previous Congresses, and (4) the National Referral Center File, for information on selected research organizations that answer inquiries from the public.

You are instructed on the use of the computer in the Computer Catalog Center.

Digital Optical Disk and Analog Videodisk Technology. Using special terminals located in some of the reading rooms, you can identify articles whose text has been put on disk, view them on the terminal screen, and print them out immediately. Analog videodisk technology permits storage of up to 108,000 low-resolution color or black-and-white images on the two sides of a disk. It serves to preserve from decay not only print but also nonprint materials (i.e., prints, photographs, motion pictures), to reduce retrieval time, to provide unlimited storage capacity, and to eliminate the "not-on-shelf" and "missing" reports common to all libraries.

Brief Bibliography

Most guides to libraries and research use the bibliographic approach; some deal with special fields, such as John E. Pemberton, *British Official Publications* (Oxford; Pergamon, 1973), and Judith S. Robinson, *Subject Guide to U.S. Government Reference Sources* (Littleton, CO: Libraries Unlimited, 1985). Others list books under subject of research, such as David Bryant, *Finding Information the Library Way: A Guide to Reference Sources* (Hamden, Conn; Library Professional pubs., 1987), and Grant W. Morse, *Concise Guide to Library Research* (New York: Fleet Academic, 1975), or by specific subject department, such as the following:

LAW

Cohen, Morris, and Robert Behring. *How to Find the Law* (St. Paul: West, 1983), or Banks, Margaret. *Using a Law Library,* 4th ed. (Toronto: Carswell, 1985).

MEDICINE

Morton, Leslie. *How to Use a Medical Library,* 4th ed. (London: Heinemann, 1964).

GENEALOGY

Doane, Gilbert. *Searching for Your Ancestors* (Minneapolis: University of Minnesota, 1980).

Stevenson, Noel. *Search and Research; the Researcher's Handbook; A Guide to Official Records and Library Sources for Investigators, Historians, Genealogists, Lawyers and Librarians* (Salt Lake City: Desert Book, 1973).

General guides like Eugene P. Sheehy, *Guide to Reference Books,* 10th ed. (Chicago; ALA, 1986) will provide a list of the major reference works in most fields.

Rather than providing a lengthy bibliography of the publications referred to in this book, I include a brief list of reference books of immediate usefulness by subject department to give you an idea of the kind of book you can expect the department to have.

SCIENCE AND TECHNOLOGY

Computer Abstracts, 1956–

Dictionary of Organic Compounds, 5th ed. and Supplement, (New York: Chapman and Hall, 1982).

Dictionary of Organometallic Compounds, annual supplements, (New York: Chapman and Hall, 1984).

Encyclopedia of Chemical Processing and Design (New York: Marcel Decker, 1976–   ).

Kirk-Othmer Encyclopedia of Chemical Technology, 3rd ed., vols. 1–24, Index, and Supplements (New York: Wiley, 1984).

Mitchell Manuals for Automotive Professionals (San Diego: Mitchell, 1981).

Sweets Catalog: Products for Industrial Construction and Renovation 4 vols. annually (a collection of manufacturers' catalogs).

ECONOMICS

Dictionary of Occupational Titles (Washington, D.C.: U.S. Labor Dept., 1977).

Editor and Publisher. Market Guide, annual (New York: 1924–   ).

Encyclopedia of Business Information Sources (Detroit: Gale, 1986).

(Munn's) *Encyclopedia of Banking and Finance* (Boston: Bankers Publishing, 1983).

Index of Economic Articles in Journals and Collective Volumes, annual (Homewood, Ill.: R. D. Irwin, 1884/1924–   ).

Standard Directory of Advertisers, annual (New York: National Register ·Publishing, 1964–   ).

Standard & Poor's Register of Corporations, Directors and Executives, annual (New York: Standard & Poor's Corp., 1928–   ).

Standard Rate and Data Service (Skokie, Ill.: 1919–   ) (a series of separate publications published irregularly).

Thomas' Register of American Manufacturers and Thomas' Register Catalog File, annual (New York: Thomas Publishing Co., 1909 –   ).

HUMANITIES

Access; the Supplementary Index to Periodicals (Syracuse, N.Y.: 1975 –   ).

Bibliography of American Literature (by) J. N. Blanck (New Haven: Yale University Press, 1955–83).

Cambridge Bibliography of English Literature (Cambridge: Cambridge University Press, 1940–77).

Celebrity Register (New York: International Inc., 1986).

Cole's Cross Reference Directory, annual (New York).

Encyclopedia of Black America (New York: McGraw-Hill, 1981).

Encyclopedia of World Art (New York: McGraw-Hill, 1981).

(Bartlett's) *Familiar Quotations* (Boston: Little, Brown, 1980).

Granger's Index to Poetry (New York: Columbia University Press, 1986).

Guinness Sports Record Book, annual (New York: Sterling, 1956 –   ).

Handbook of Latin American Studies, 2 vols. annually (Austin: University of Texas).

Harvard Guide to American History (Cambridge: Belknap Press, 1974).

Holidays and Anniversaries of the World (Detroit: Gale, 1985).

Hotel and Motel Red Book, annual (New York: American Hotel Association, 1886–   ).

Literary Market Place, annual (New York: Bowker, 1940–   ).

MLA Handbook for Writers of Research Papers, 2d ed. (by) Joseph Gibaldi, Walter S. Achtert (New York: Modern Language Association, 1984) ("a set of conventions governing the written presentation of research").

MLA International Bibliography of Books and Articles on the Modern

Languages and Literatures, annual (New York: Modern Language Association, 1921–   ).

Martindale-Hubbell Law Directory, annual (New York: Martindale-Hubbell, 1931–   ).

National Union Catalog, pre-1956 imprints, 685 vols. (London: Mansell, 1968–80).

Psychological Abstracts, monthly (Lancaster, Pa.: 1927–   ).

The Reader's Adviser; a Layman's Guide to Literature (New York: Bowker, 1986).

Scott's Standard Postage Stamp Catalog, annual (New York: Scott Publishing, 1867–   ).

A Short-title Catalogue of Books Printed in England, Scotland and Ireland, Wales, and British America. 1641–1700, 3 vols. (New York: Columbia University Press, 1945–51).

Who's Who in America, A Biographical Dictionary of Notable Living Men and Women, biennial (Chicago: Marquis, 1899–   ).

Working Press of the Nation, annual in 5 vols. (New York: Farrell Publishing, 1945–   ) (a catalog of newspaper, magazine, T.V. and radio, feature writing, photographer, internal publications).

World of Learning, annual (London: Europa Publications, 1946–   ).

Index

157